SUB-LIEUTENANT

1 H.M.S. *T——*

SUB-LIEUTENANT

A PERSONAL RECORD OF THE WAR AT SEA

by

LUDOVIC KENNEDY

Illustrated by Photographs

LONDON

B. T. BATSFORD LTD.

15 North Audley Street, W.1

First Published October 1942

MADE AND PRINTED IN GREAT BRITAIN FOR THE PUBLISHERS,
B. T. BATSFORD LTD., LONDON, BY WILLIAM CLOWES AND SONS, LTD.,
LONDON AND BECCLES

TO MY SHIPMATES

PUBLISHERS' NOTE

This book is the record of a very young man's life at Eton and Oxford, and then for two years on active service with a Destroyer Flotilla of the Home Fleet. As such it needs no explanation except, perhaps, that its author is 22 and now a Lieutenant R.N.V.R., and that it was written, to use his own words, "as a hobby to pass many dreary hours at sea—in the Atlantic, the North Sea and the Arctic; in England, Scotland, Ireland, Iceland, the Faroes, Spitzbergen and Russia." A section pays a tribute to his father who, as Captain of the *Rawalpindi*, was lost in the first, and one of the most gallant, naval actions of this war.

ACKNOWLEDGMENT

Most of the illustrations (figs. 1, 3, 4, 6, 7, 8, 9, 11, 12, 13, 15, 16, 18, 19, 21, 22, 23 and 25) are from photographs taken by the Author. Of the remainder, fig 2 was kindly supplied by the Peninsular and Oriental Steam Navigation Co.; figs. 14, 20 and 24 are from British Official War Photographs, and are reproduced by permission of the Ministry of Information; fig. 10 is by Central Press; and fig. 17 by Associated Press.

CONTENTS

CHAPTER ONE

POP-ROOM

I

The first years of my life are of no importance.   At the age of nine, I was packed off to a preparatory school in the South of England, and for the next four years led the usual life of a preparatory-school boy.   I indulged in midnight feasts and was periodically beaten.   I had mumps, chicken-pox and measles, and I was quite often sick from over-eating.   I hero-worshipped a boy called Campbell II, and, a little later, had rather queer dreams about one of the matrons, a most glamorous creature.

By the winter of 1932 I was a school prefect, and captain of a dormitory.   My dormitory was called " Nelson," and I don't suppose there's been such a bad dormitory in the school before or since.

At the end of each term a prize was awarded to the captain of the most efficient dormitory—that is, the one which had scored the fewest bad marks.   Bad marks were given by the matrons for untidy beds, broken crockery and general uncleanliness or inefficiency.   Three bad marks constituted a bad point ; when a boy had scored that, it was the privilege of the captain of his dormitory to give him " one up " on the bare behind.   This was carried out in the presence of the headmaster with what was known as " the juiciest hair-brush in the school," borrowed for the occasion from whoever happened to be its owner.

There were only five boys in " Nelson," including myself, but between us we amassed, by the end of the term, a total of twenty-three bad marks, or nearly eight points.   Eight of the marks were caused by a bat which found its way into the dormitory one night after " lights out."   We spent an amusing half-hour chasing this animal, egged on by one Pemberton, who had a secret store of " tuck " and was offering four toffee-drops to the first person who captured it.

Pemberton's zeal was his undoing.   He was leaping about his bed, shouting encouragement, when the springs collapsed beneath him and he fell sideways on to his washstand.   The result was that Pemberton got six bad marks for breaking his jug, his basin, his toothglass, his commode and two springs of his bed; I got two bad marks for permitting " hooliganism "; —total, eight marks.   The next day I beat Pemberton twice and the Head beat me once.   The bat escaped.

The next term I went to Eton.

II

My father was driving the car, with my mother beside him. I sat in a corner at the back, a small, unhappy figure, trying to prevent my luggage from squashing me.

We passed through Slough, and soon Agar's Plough came into sight on the left.   In a few minutes we would be in Eton, and I knew that I could no longer keep to myself the question which had been troubling me all the afternoon.

" Do they bully new boys much ? " I asked.

" Rather ! " said my father in his bluff, naval way.   " Give you an awful rough time of it ! "   I knew he didn't mean it by the way he laughed, but I wasn't reassured.

" No, darling, they don't bully little boys at school any more," said my mother.   " That's a thing of the past."

" You'll be all right, old boy," said my father.

The sight of my house-master did nothing to diminish my fears.   " Sam " was a tall, bulky man with broad shoulders and a bull's neck.   He was almost bald on top, and wore horn-rimmed spectacles through which his eyes glared terrifyingly.

I don't think any of we Lower Boys liked Sam, nor did we hate him; our feelings towards him were compounded of fear and respect.   He had a habit of entering your room after " lights out " and third-degreeing you with a torch.   Also, he was one of the few house-masters who beat their boys—with a cane on the bare buttock. All the same, there was not one of us who was not sorry to hear of his tragic death on the Piz Roseg the next summer. He understood more about growing boys and their difficulties than anyone I have met. If a boy was in trouble, Sam would find out what the trouble was, help him, and finally rid him of it. During the fifteen years he was a house-master at Eton, only one boy was expelled from his house, and that for an offence for which there was no alternative punishment.

For any serious offence, Sam would beat the boy and then " jaw " him for an hour or so every night for the next three weeks. It was an unorthodox method but, like other unorthodox methods, it worked.

III

By the Easter half of 1938 I had risen to a position in the school which entitled me to many small privileges and a certain authority. I was in my house library, and I could fag. Because I was the only house colour, I automatically became Captain of Games. I was a member of the Shakespeare Society, a body of six scholars and six oppidans which drank coffee and read Shakespeare's plays in the Provost's study every Tuesday evening. I belonged to the Political Society, which drank coffee and listened to statesmen and politicians in the Vice-Provost's study every Wednesday evening. Being a Scot, I joined the Caledonian Society and danced reels with my fellow-countrymen in School Hall, whenever it was available. Best of all, I was elected to " Pop."

Shane Leslie has said of Pop (or, as it is officially called, " The Eton Society ") : " The three most exclusive bodies in the world are the College of Cardinals, the Bench of the Supreme Court of the United States of America, and Pop. Of these three, a young Etonian would infinitely prefer to be in Pop."

To wear the fancy waistcoat and winged collar—the stamp of Pop membership—is the dream of the ambitious Etonian.

3

The authority of Pop is supreme and unchallengeable; its privileges are varied and many. A Pop may link arms with his friends in the street, and walk on the left-hand pavement of the High Street. He may wear khaki shorts instead of the standard grey ones. In the summer, he may bathe in a stretch of water slightly less filthy than the rest of the Thames. He may wear braid on his coat, sealing-wax on his hat, and a flower in his button-hole. . . .

That Easter half passed pleasantly. Having been more or less kicked out of the O.T.C. for placing a "No Thoroughfare" notice on the Tidworth-Salisbury road at the last summer camp, I joined the newly-formed Air Squadron. Instead of attending the Corps Parades on Monday mornings, we assembled in a classroom in New Schools and listened to lectures by officers from the R.A.F. Station at Northolt. On field days, instead of rolling about the Surrey heather, we were taken to Northolt in an R.A.F. lorry. In the morning we visited the hangars, workshops and repair sheds; then came a first-class lunch in the officers' mess, followed by quarter of an hour in the air in an Avro Tutor. An instructional film, and tea, completed the day.

We were at Northolt the day Squadron-Leader Gillan flew there from Edinburgh in three-quarters of an hour. This astonished us, but seemed to make little impression on the station officers.

In the middle of the half, I went to Oxford for four days to sit for the Christ Church Scholarship examination. I don't really know why I went, because my chances of getting a scholarship were infinitesimal; but my father had said that the least I could do was to fail, which I did.

The examination was held in the lovely Hall of Christ Church. We sat in alphabetical order. I was sandwiched between a German called Kuenstler and a Pole called Kaufmann; in front of me was an Irishman called Keogh, and next to him an Arab called Kavak. Kuenstler and Kaufmann wrote like men possessed. Keogh wrote or chewed his pen alternately every five minutes. Kennedy wrote a word or two now and then, but Kavak never wrote at all. He glared around him, and I had a feeling that he was going to knife someone.

Kaufmann got a scholarship; but I never heard of Kuenstler, Keogh or Kavak again. After four days in their company, I was glad to get back to the friendly surroundings of Eton.

IV

My last summer half at Eton was one of the happiest times of my life. I had passed the Christ Church entrance exam during the holidays; I was Captain of Games in my tutors; and I was in Pop. Compared with many of my associates, whose bedroom walls were festooned with lists and colours, mine was a modest achievement. But it was good enough.

At the beginning of the half, Billy, John, Dick and I revived a society which had been extinct for two years, the Thursday Breakfast Club. Each Thursday morning, after early school, we went " down town " to Tap, a famous Eton public-house, where Mr. Hobbs provided us with a huge breakfast of porridge and cream, fish, eggs and bacon, coffee, toast and marmalade; after a fortnight we cut out the fish as it tended to make us late for chapel. We took it in turns to invite a guest, usually a fellow member of Pop. Long after the cups and saucers in the House dining-room had been cleared away we lingered over our coffee and toast.

The Political Society flourished as it had never done before, thanks to its President, Billy E——, who attracted to Eton such public men as Lord Baldwin, Lord Halifax, Major Attlee, Mr. Eden and Lord Londonderry. Lord Baldwin came to Eton soon after he had been made a peer. In his speech of welcome, Billy twice referred to him as *Mr.* Baldwin. The first time he slurred over his mistake; the second time he stopped and apologised.

" That's all right," said Lord Baldwin, " I'm quite new."

The Shakespeare Society continued to hold its pleasant after-dinner meetings; the Caledonian Society danced more frequently. Henley came and the Winchester match, then Lord's; and those of us who were leaving realised with a pang that there was only a fortnight to go.

Lord's was followed by the House cricket-matches. We drew a house slightly worse than ourselves, and amassed a score of 301 for the loss of two wickets. I made 77 not out, the highest score of my cricketing career; but for the spirit of public school sportsmanship, which forced me to declare the innings closed, I should probably have made a hundred. In the second round we were soundly beaten.

I went in for the Annual Poetry Prize, and came in second for the second year running, which rather annoyed me. I might have done something in the Declamation Prize if I had not memorised the wrong passage from the Bible.

With the last week came a succession of farewell parties— leaving breakfasts every morning, at which we ploughed through the whole rigmarole of porridge, fish and eggs; tea-parties which were not quite so strenuous; and dinner-parties. There was a dinner with my tutor, at which we refilled our port glasses while he was taking prayers; a dinner with the headmaster and the Vice-Provost; and dinners with masters with whom I had struck up friendships during my five years at Eton.

Finally, there was the business of photographs: House photographs, Pop photographs, and photographs of one another which would appear in our racks marked "R.S.V.P." I have a drawer at home to-day full of photographs signed "Peter," "Mike" or "John," with the date, "1938," in the bottom right-hand corner. Some of the Peters, Mikes and Johns are dead, some are prisoners of war. Many are serving in distant corners of the world. There are few whom I am likely to see again.

CHAPTER TWO

COMMON-ROOM

I

The year I spent at Oxford was a pleasant one. Whether it did me any good is another matter.

I did the same silly things which thousands of young men have done before me, and will do after me. I fell in love—an event which took up a large part of my time and income. I learnt to like alcohol, and to hold it. I made many friends, became a member of several clubs, and went to parties. The rest of the time I worked.

The silliest thing I did was to start a roulette-board. My room at Christ Church was in a corner of Peck Quad, adjoining an unused lecture-room. Here there was a very fine oak table, which my roulette cloth fitted like a glove.

Every Friday night a party assembled in my rooms ; I was the croupier. I said " Faîtes vos jeux, messieurs," " Rien ne va plus," and wielded my rake most professionally. The money rolled in, because most of my customers followed a system which sooner or later broke down. I bought a gramophone, a sofa and goodness knows what else out of the proceeds. But one evening it seemed that the systems couldn't fail. I lost more than I care to think about, and next day L. Kennedy's roulette company went into liquidation.

There are a number of social and sporting clubs at Oxford. There is the Gridiron, where they used to give you a first-class lunch for one-and-sixpence, and the best Pimms I have tasted for nearly treble that price. There is the Carlton, in George Street, the home of the Conservatives, and Vincent's, the home of the sportsmen. The most select is the Bullingdon, to be a member of which you must be rich, " well-born " or addicted

17

to blood sports. The first of these attributes was a sufficient claim to membership in my day, though most of the members possessed at least two of them.

Connected with the Bullingdon was Loder's, a Christ Church dining club. It was founded some time in the Middle Ages as a Bible-reading society—a scarcely credible fact to anyone who attended one of its meetings in 1938. It held one meeting a week, at eight o'clock on Sunday evening, when the members (there were about a dozen) assembled in the Bullingdon rooms to eat and drink largely. During dinner nobody drank much. It was not until dessert had been cleared, and the " Silver Lady " had been placed before the President, that drinking began in earnest.

The " Silver Lady " was a silver model of a young woman dressed in the costume of the last century. A voluminous bustle curved outwards from her waist until it reached the level of her feet, where it formed a support for the rest of her body. The bustle was hollow inside and held about a quarter of a pint of champagne. Above her head the lady held a pitcher about the size of a thimble, so balanced that, however much you turned her body vertically, the pitcher retained its equilibrium.

At the cry of " Lady for so and so," she was turned upside down and her bustle and the pitcher filled with champagne. The victim had to clasp the lady's waist between the fore-finger and thumb of his right hand, raise the bustle to his lips and, at the word " Go " from the President, try to swallow the contents of both bustle and pitcher in one gulp as quickly as possible. He was not allowed to touch the pitcher with his hands, with the result that most of its contents spilled over his shirt-front.

" Rotten ! " the President would say. " Fifteen seconds ! "

The victim was generally too exhausted to care whether he had taken fifteen seconds or fifty. The record time, and one which is not likely to be bettered, was made in my day by Alec S——. He did it in six.

Another Oxford Club to which I belonged, but not for

long, was the O.U.D.S. The term I joined, three one-act plays were written, acted and produced by members. The construction, plots, dialogue and characters of these plays were so grotesque that it passed my imagination how the producer had the nerve to put them on. I played the part of a butler in one, the only character who spoke ten consecutive words of sense. After that I resigned. The next term they produced " The Duchess of Malfi " in the garden of Worcester College. The stage was set on a wooden platform floating on the lake. I believe this sank during one performance, providing the audience with an excuse to go home.

By the end of my first term I realised that I had done very little to prepare myself for the Pass Mod Examinations. I began to work in earnest, but my after-dinner studies were generally interrupted by the activities of others. There was one young man who insisted on blowing a hunting horn outside my window every night ; the contents of a water-jug used to silence him effectively. In another corner of the quad a party gathered nightly to sing Austrian folk-songs to the accompaniment of an accordion.

One evening, while this frightful sing-song was in progress and I was tearing the corners off the pages of Pliny in despair, another party arrived to play a golf match. They set to work, and the sound of splintering glass soon reverberated through the quadrangle. One bright lad announced that he was going to drive a ball over the roof of the library, a building about 150 feet high which faced the open side of the quad. If he had tried in daytime, sober, with a niblick, he might or might not have succeeded. As it was, he tried on a dark night, plastered, with a mashie.

He addressed the ball unsteadily for several minutes ; then, with a resounding smack, sent it straight through one of the library windows. I learnt the next morning that the ball had continued its flight across the library until it had hit an historic oil painting, which it had penetrated neatly before coming to rest among a pile of books.

With these distractions, it was not surprising that I failed to pass the examinations.

II

The summer of 1939 was my best time at Oxford. Parties succeeded each other continuously—parties in people's rooms, parties on the river ; parties at Newbury and Newmarket and Cambridge ; parties at Loder's, and a tremendous party at the annual Bullingdon dinner. This took place in a barn eight miles outside the city, as it was forbidden within the precincts, and we went there in taxis. On the return journey my host, Alastair, uplifted by champagne, harangued the taxi-driver steadily on his bad driving. At last the man could stand it no longer.

"Why don't *you* 'ave a go, if you know so ruddy much abaht it ? " he said.

That was what Alastair had been waiting for. He pushed the driver from his seat and took the wheel himself. Not without danger, he brought us to the Canterbury Gate of Christ Church, outside which there is a lamp-post in the middle of the street. Alastair drove round and round that lamp-post at an increasing speed until the moment came when taxi and lamp-post, attracted to each other beyond endurance, connected. The damage, I think, came to thirty pounds.

There were evenings when two or three of us would slip up to London to attend one of the nightly " deb-dances," and return to Oxford in the early hours of the next morning. If our Oxford parties had little justification, the London Season parties seemed to have less. At least our parties were for the most part spontaneous.

There is an Oxford saying that undergraduates who get Firsts are the friends of the examiners, those who get Seconds are the people who work, those who get Thirds are the people who don't work, and those who get Fourths are the friends of the examiners. I was not working for a degree, only for a pass ; but I hoped, as I entered the examination hall in the last week of term, that the examiner was a friend of mine. I need have had no fears. I had determined not to fail a third time, and I found no difficulty in answering the questions put before me. Before the examination was over I knew that I had passed.

Early in the morning, two days later, I loaded my belongings into my car and wished my scout good-bye. Tom Quad looked very beautiful in the early morning light. The sun threw long shadows across the lawns ; an air of tranquillity and repose seemed to infuse each building. " Good-bye, Clifford," I said ; " have a good holiday."

" Good-bye, sir," said Clifford ; " see you in October."

But a long time was to pass, and many things were to happen, before I saw Clifford again.

CHAPTER THREE

LAST VACATION

I

On Islay, under the shadow of Ben Bhan and three miles from Bridgend, stands the farmhouse of Cean-na-Croich. Here, for the past four years, I had spent a month of the summer holidays with my family. We were looked after by two admirable sisters, the Misses Taylor, who fed us like kings and to whom nothing was too much trouble. They were very dear women.

I spent most of my time that summer with my father. In spite of the fact that our views on most matters seldom coincided, we had a profound understanding of one another. He came of the old school of naval officers which has learnt to acknowledge discipline and self-control as the first qualities in a man. He had a code of honour, a fixed belief in what was right and wrong, and a pre-determined viewpoint on every matter which no power on earth could change. Fresh from Oxford, where few people hold the same view on any subject for more than a few weeks, I would propound the most exaggerated theories to him. But to argue with my father was like arguing with a brick wall; there was no matter on which he did not hold a precise and definite opinion. As he had held the same opinions for the past forty years there was no likelihood that my immature convictions would alter them.

We found our deepest understanding through two sports, shooting and fishing, a love for which he had instilled in me at an early age. He was an expert fisherman and a good shot. Each year he took a small shoot between the Rhinns of Islay and Portnahaven. Cladville, it was called, and its owner, a stout Scottish farmer, referred to it as " the piece moor." The " piece moor " provided us with many fruitful days of shooting. The bags were never large, but they were varied—

grouse and a hare or two from the moor itself; snipe and occasionally a duck from a strip of marsh below the farm-house; pigeon and plover from the cliffs which marked the seaward boundary of the shoot; and, later on, a few partridges.

On other days we would go fishing in Finlaggan, Staoisha or Ardnahoe; or sometimes we would strike up into the hills to fish some mountain loch marked on the map, meeting my mother and sisters for tea at a rendezvous on the other side. This was the sort of expedition my father loved; it gratified his desire to explore unknown territory with compass and map.

I shall never forget, one wet evening, sitting alone with him in the house. He pulled an envelope out of his pocket which bore the crown of the Admiralty. " I haven't shown you this before," he said, " because when I first received it there didn't seem any likelihood of it happening. It's the best news I've had for some time."

I unfolded the letter and began to read. It contained several long paragraphs written in official language, but I soon had the gist of it. *In the event of hostilities, would my father be prepared to take command of an armed merchant cruiser?* I knew my father, and understood his excitement.

There is a school of naval officers (I have met some of them during this war) who are embittered at an institution which has no use for their services as senior officers. Their bitterness is understandable. When you have devoted the best years of your life to a service which equips you for no other calling and flings you out when it has done with you, you are entitled to a complaint.

Shortly after the end of the last war the Government, for reasons of economy, decided to reduce drastically the number of senior naval officers. The " Geddes Axe " fell, and my father was placed on the retired list. He was bitterly disappointed, but at no time embittered. He accepted the measure as a necessity for the good of his country, put the matter out of his head, and turned his hand to politics.

But he could never altogether escape the weight of the blow. Meeting old Navy friends, hearing Navy talk from past shipmates, any incident which brought him in touch with the Navy during the post-war years, reminded him with a pang of his yearning for the sea. The thrill of conning a big ship, of ordering her ways, of influencing the lives of her crew, were memories which he could not forget easily. When he received this letter from the Admiralty, he saw himself in an instant standing once more on the bridge of his own ship.

I finished reading the letter and handed it back to him. He turned to me with an almost youthful exuberance.

" I shall be sixty next week, old boy," he said, " and they still have enough faith in me to offer me a ship. Eighteen years on the beach, and they offer me a ship ! Gosh, what a chance ! *What* a chance ! "

It was to come sooner than he, or any of us, expected.

II

I went to Skye at the end of August for the Portree Gathering.

There is a bay on the east coast of the island called Loch Eillort, where at low tide you can pick as many oysters as you can carry. On the 1st September, the opening day of the oyster season, my hostess took us there.

It was a boisterous, chilly day—the kind of day you would prefer to spend indoors, but which you enjoy almost more than any other kind once you have set foot outside. With the three men and four girls of the house party, I paddled contentedly among the rocks all the morning, picking up an oyster here and there but finding more often than not that the big shells from the bottom of the pools were empty husks.

We lunched in a little wood beside the road, under the shadow of the Cuillins, and continued the hunt. By the end of the day the bag amounted to nearly two hundred oysters.

I went down to the boathouse when we got back that evening, and was tinkering with one of the sails when I heard a step behind me. Turning, I saw Harry, a fellow guest. He looked grave.

" Well, Ludo," he said, " the war's on. Germany invaded Poland this morning."

It was a relief anyway, after so many days of waiting, of listening to one news bulletin after another. The last five days had been a strain. We went on as though nothing was happening in the outside world, pretending that nothing was happening, but knowing in our hearts that, on the outcome of those five days, the fate of the world was balanced.

That night and the next morning various members of the house party left, in response to telegrams, to rejoin their units. Next day, too, feeling that the peaceful island was no place for me in such times, I packed my belongings and took to the road.

How lovely Skye was looking that morning—so tranquil, so at ease, so typically Scotland ! The sky was a clear, soft blue against which the outlines of the Cuillins stood up sharply. At Loch Alsh, which I crossed by the ferry to the mainland, little boats were making their way leisurely across the Sound of Sleat. Seagulls wheeled in the crisp morning air ; oyster-catchers and sandpipers darted across the shores, uttering their weird cries. In a wayside loch trout were on the move, their dark fins rippling the surface of the water.

Driving through Stirling late that night, I saw for the first time the shape of things to come. Not a light showed ; the town was wrapped in darkness.

At my grandmother's house in Edinburgh, where I arrived in the early hours of the morning, I found a letter from my mother. She told me that my father had flown south two days before to take command of his ship. There goes one man anyway, I thought, who is really happy !

Next day we listened to Chamberlain's solemn speech on the wireless. Then the sirens sounded for the first time, and we stole down to the cellar where, hand in hand, we stayed petrified until the All-Clear.

After that I went upstairs and wrote a letter to the Admiralty, volunteering my services. The reply came four months later (when I had been in naval uniform for nine weeks), regretting that there were at present no vacancies and advising me to try again in six months' time.

A few days later I had news of my father's ship. She was a P. and O. liner of seventeen thousand tons, and my father had joined her already. At present she was in dock being converted into a man-of-war; her luxury fittings were being removed and six-inch guns installed on her upper decks. In six weeks she would be ready for sea. In six weeks she would hoist the White Ensign and steam to her patrol, a warship of the Royal Navy.

Her name was *Rawalpindi*.

CHAPTER FOUR

H.M.S. *KING ALFRED*

I

A fortnight later I saw my father on board *Rawalpindi*.

I have never seen him so happy ; he was like a child who has been given a new toy. During tea in his cabin, a luxurious room behind the bridge, he kept jumping up to discuss with dockyard officials alterations they were making to the ship's structure ; or one of his officers would come to him with a batch of papers for scrutiny and signature. Afterwards he took me around the ship. We visited each cabin, each compartment, from the boat-deck to the engine-room, while he explained the alterations the ship was undergoing, many of which he had himself authorised. We would often stop while he straightened out some problem raised by one of the workmen.

His enthusiasm was unbounded, his pride immense. I knew then that the disappointments which had been rankling for the past eighteen years had vanished. They were forgotten in his passionate interest and pride in his new command.

Before I left, he showed me the guns lying on the jetty, waiting to be fitted. Big, powerful creatures they looked, their snouts pointing threateningly to the sky. Across the shield of each gun was scribbled in thick white letters RAWALPINDI.

These were the guns about which my father wrote later to a friend, " They have given me some guns, good guns, and I am going to use them."

That was the last time I saw my father. But he used his guns all right.

II

In the middle of October, as a result of an interview with the Joint Universities Recruiting Board at Oxford, I was commissioned in the Navy as a Probationary Temporary Sub-Lieutenant R.N.V.R., and appointed to H.M.S. *King Alfred*, additional.

H.M.S. *King Alfred* is at Brighton. I was billeted in an hotel in Fourth Avenue, whose inmates were mostly old ladies and retired colonels. I shared a room with a man whose name I cannot remember, but who was the dullest man I have ever met. Fortunately he complained of my flow of language during the night (I talk and shout in my sleep regularly) and, after a few days, left me.

Shortly after reporting at *King Alfred* I was brought up before the Commanding Officer, Captain P——, Royal Navy.

" You're Kennedy ? " he said. " I knew your father in the last war. I hear he's got the *Rawalpindi* now."

I was surprised that he knew anything about me. We talked for a few moments, then he asked.

" How old are you ? "

" Nineteen, sir," I answered. " I shall be twenty in a fortnight's time."

" In that case," he said, " you'll have to be a midshipman. You were born a fortnight too late."

So I was disrated to midshipman, and shipped two hideous red tabs on the lapels of my monkey-jacket.

Training at *King Alfred* was of an elementary sort. We were taught the first principles of the conduct of naval warfare. We learned the rules of the road and the laws of navigation. We did gun drill on an ancient weapon, and listened to a Chief Petty Officer explaining the intricacies of torpedoes and depth charges. We were taught to send and receive messages in morse and semaphore and, in an adjacent park, did field training. . . .

III

H.M.S. *Rawalpindi*,
c/o G.P.O.
London.

My dear Boy,

I have several letters of yours to answer. Some I fear are rather old, but that cannot be helped, as I have no time when we are in harbour for perhaps a couple of days, and then we are at sea for several.

Mummy will have told you of the two days we had when we spent a night at the cottage—most comfortable—then lunch with Ga finishing with a flick in Glasgow before we were off again. This we hope to repeat, but our future is always uncertain.

I was very pleased to hear how well you shot with Uncle Tom. You mentioned this to me yourself, and I also heard it from Beechwood. What you must learn now is the driven bird low and high, though I don't know when you will get any practice at this. Once you get the knack, you will be all right, but it is quite different to walking up. Your gun seems to fit you admirably. . . .

Yes, I did shake hands with the King when he visited the Fleet, and we had quite a chat. His equerry, Harold Campbell, I know well, and I was glad to meet him and others whom I have not seen for years. It's very amusing meeting some of the bigwigs now who were contemporaries of mine. They are all very jolly and welcoming.

One full Admiral, whom I had not met before, remarked in conversation, " I see you have the China medal. What ship were you in ? " to which I replied that I was a sub in the *Barfleur*, when he said that he was a midshipman in the *Endymion*. . . .

While writing the above, the bridge reported that our pet iceberg was again in sight, a formidable, ghost-like object, so I thought this a good opportunity to do some more gunnery. We had a very spirited attack on it this afternoon

5

at long range, and with considerable motion on the ship, which made it difficult but very instructive. . . .

What I want to know is how long you will remain a midshipman, what work and general training you do (this your next letter will probably tell me), when you are likely to get a sea appointment and what form it is likely to take.

Another thing I want to know is the question of your finances. Tell me frankly, have you any debts now or are they all paid off? And if they are, pray do not involve yourself in any that you cannot meet. What pay will you get, what will your messing cost, what do they allow you for uniform? All this I want to know, and then I will see what allowance to give you. Now is the time when we must all live as economically as possible. Income-tax has soared up, and I don't know what I shall be doing, if anything, once we have seen this show through.

Best of luck, my dear fellow,

POP.

IV

I went to Bedford in the middle of November for a special course.

The middle of November is about the worst time of the year to visit Bedford. The River Ouse overflows and floods the surrounding countryside, which is as flat as a billiard-table, a foot deep. Blankets of fog descend on the town, lingering for days. The atmosphere is damp and not very healthy. There are no industries of much importance in Bedford so far as I know, and there are certainly no attractions.

I was billeted in St. Mary's Abbey Hotel, an old building which exactly fitted my conception of the Abbey in *The Black Arrow*. My bedroom overlooked the road; my friend Bill R——'s was next to it. What Bill found to amuse him in Bedford I don't know, but he would set out early in the evening in my car, which he abused abominably, and return in the early hours of the morning, having forgotten his

key, by way of the ivy and my bedroom window. One night
the ivy came away in his hands and he smashed a wooden
cill which jutted over the front door. The next day the
proprietor presented him with a fat bill for damages. After
that Bill took pains to remember his key.

On the evening of Sunday, the 26th November, I motored
along the Ampthill road to dine with a friend of my father's.
Before me lay a good dinner, good company and a comfortable house ; behind me the memory of forty-eight hours I had
spent revisiting Oxford. The place had changed strangely.
Of my contemporaries, there was only a handful left ; of my
friends, none. Only Clifford, whose last words when he had
said good-bye to me in July had been, " See you again in
October, sir," remembered me. Even he had changed ; he
seemed older, and more responsible of his duties.

" It's terrible 'ere now, sir," he had said. " Nothing but
black men and medicos, *and* an 'ole crowd of foreigners from
other colleges. I'd give a lot to 'ave the old days back, sir,
parties and all. . . ."

Arrived at Ampthill, we dined and went into the library
to hear the news on the wireless. It's queer how detachedly
one listens to the news nowadays—a result, I suppose, of
listening to it so often. I was smoking a cigarette and drum-
ming my fingers on the table, not concentrating on what was
being said, when one word struck a chord in my brain and
made me sit bolt upright on my chair. Then the subconscious
part of my brain transmitted the last few words to the
conscious part.

" The Secretary of the Admiralty," came the impassive
voice of the announcer, " regrets to announce the loss of the
Armed Merchant Cruiser *Rawalpindi*. H.M.S. *Rawalpindi* was
an ex-P. and O. liner of seventeen thousand tons. . . ."

The voice drifted on, but I did not listen. For I knew then
that my father was dead. . . .

My father came of the old and noble breed of naval officers
who hold honour dearer than life. To them, the achievements
of a ship are due to the resource of her Captain. If a Captain

should hazard his ship, whether the blame is attributable to him or not, it is his duty to go down with her.

To-day, a younger school decries this theory. It recognises that the Captain should be the last to leave his ship, but insists that, while there is an opportunity for him to get away, he should take it, and thus be of further service to his country. That is a reasonable view, of course, but one cannot well criticise such men as Captain Makeig-Jones, of the *Courageous*, who remained alone on the bridge of his ship saluting the flag as she went down.

I went over to the telephone, and eventually was put through to the Admiralty. A long pause, then a voice said: " The Captain ? No, I'm afraid he's gone. . . ."

CHAPTER FIVE

H.M.S. *RAWALPINDI*

During the last war, the Tenth Cruiser Squadron, consisting of armed passenger and merchant ships, formed what was known as the Northern Patrol. The limits of this patrol stretched from the north of Scotland to the Faroes, then south of Iceland to the north coast of Norway. Its object was two-fold : to intercept German merchant shipping endeavouring to return home *via* the North Sea, and to report the presence of enemy warships breaking out into the Atlantic to raid our convoys.

So successfully was this duty executed that, on the outbreak of this war, the squadron was reformed, and within a few weeks many armed merchant cruisers were at sea. One of the first to commission was *Rawalpindi*. By the beginning of October, 1939, she was patrolling the desolate waters south of Iceland.

Her complement was 39 officers and about 210 ratings. Of the officers, only one, Mr. French, was on the active service list of the Royal Navy. With the exception of the Captain and the First Lieutenant, Lieutenant-Commander Molson, Royal Navy, all the other officers were drawn from the Naval and Naval Volunteer Reserves. The men, with few exceptions, were reservists or pensioners. Many of the officers and men had served in the ship under the Red Ensign.

The service of the Northern Patrol is arduous and must be endured in the worst kind of weather. In winter, daylight lasts only a few hours. Blizzards and snowstorms lash the seas, and there is always a bitter, numbing cold which seems to take the breath out of the body.

Rawalpindi seems to have been a happy ship ; and the crew seem soon to have accustomed themselves to their new duties. A few days after sailing for the first patrol my father wrote home, " Everything is beginning to shape well. Molson has

33

just left me after a long talk about everyone.   We are happy
about everything and agree that in a short time we will be able
to hold our own with the others. . . .   At sea, everyone is a
different person, and the crew seem to be settling down very
well."   A few days later he wrote, " Everything in the ship
is slowly and surely shaping itself.   It has been an interesting
experiment trying to circulate the right spirit into such a
mixed crowd. . . .   The mercantile firemen, who are usually
very undisciplined, are coming quite into line and have
expressed a wish to share the same recreation room as the
seamen, to which the latter have agreed.   They don't want to
be different, a very good sign, and after my rounds this
morning, I was able to congratulate various people on the way
they had cleaned up their departments.   An excellent
atmosphere is beginning to prevail."

About himself he wrote, " I wondered from the start if I had
got too rusty.   Some things certainly were a bit strange at
first, but I feel now as if I was back in the last war and there
had been no interlude at all.   It has all come back, and I find
there is little I have forgotten.   But I feel I must make good
and I realise the responsibility of this command more than I
ever did in my former commands. . . ."

There is little opportunity for exercise on board a warship
at sea, so my father introduced a routine which he had evolved
when Commander of the battle-cruiser *New Zealand* in the last
war.   He made the men march round the decks several times
after morning prayers.   " I warned them we would do it, and
I myself led them with Molson.   Some of the mercantile men
thought it a bit of a joke till I made them run the last lap of
over 300 yards.   They were all so pumped (except me) that
they became quite subdued and appreciated that they were all
the better for it.   We will probably do it daily."

So *Rawalpindi* patrolled her station in the North Atlantic.
Although the squadron of A.M.C.'s engaged on the Northern
Patrol had no flagship (the flag of the Vice-Admiral Northern
Patrol is flown ashore), *Rawalpindi*, by virtue of her Captain's
seniority, was looked upon as the flagship.   For this reason,

2, 3 H.M.S. *RAWALPINDI* AND HER CAPTAIN

4 TRIBAL DESTROYERS IN LINE AHEAD

her crew were especially anxious to maintain the highest standard of fighting efficiency.

My father lost no opportunity to exercise the guns' crews and put in as many practice shoots as the weather allowed. " In all respects," wrote Sir Max Horton, the Vice-Admiral Commanding Northern Patrol, " *Rawalpindi*, under his command, was outstanding. The high standard he expected, and got, was reflected in the smartness and appearance of his ship and ship's company."

On her first patrol, *Rawalpindi* intercepted the German merchantman *G——*; her crew were taken prisoners. " The Captain of the *G——*," wrote my father, " was a real gentleman." Before leaving *Rawalpindi*, he wrote my father a letter thanking him for the kind and courteous treatment he and his crew had received on board, which, he said, he would never forget ; and he presented my father with his binoculars, the only possession he had saved from his ship. These were handed on to Sub-Lieutenant Anderson, the boarding officer, who has them to-day.

At the end of *Rawalpindi's* first and second patrols my father got a few days' leave, which he spent with my mother and sisters at the cottage in Perthshire. On one of these visits my mother had happened to ask him, " What would you do if you sighted the *Deutschland*? "

" Run like a hare," he had replied.

About the middle of November, *Rawalpindi* left harbour and steamed northwards on her third and last patrol. The weather was as vile as usual and, in order to pass the tedious hours, a concert-party was arranged. The first performance was held on the evening of the 22nd November ; it was a huge success. The Captain was asked to do a turn, and to everyone's surprise, agreed. He sang " Tom Bowling," and sat down amid much applause. So successful was the concert that it was decided to hold a second performance the next evening.

The following day, the 23rd, a Swedish ship was sighted, and Sub-Lieutenant Anderson, the boarding officer, was ordered to take her into a British port with an armed guard. Anderson was appearing in the concert party and had no wish to leave the ship, so he spun a coin with Lieutenant Pickersgill, the second boarding officer, to decide which of them should command the armed guard.   Anderson lost, and left the ship.

Rawalpindi continued her patrol until about 3.30 in the afternoon " when," in the words of the Admiralty *communiqué*, " she sighted an enemy ship."   My father looked at her through his glasses.   " It's the *Deutschland* all right," he said.

Action stations were rung on the alarm bells, and course was altered away.   Smoke floats were lit and thrown into the water, but unfortunately they failed to burn.   A signal was sent at once to the base reporting the enemy's position, course and speed.

The enemy warship (later evidence tends to show that it was not the *Deutschland*) closed *Rawalpindi* and made the signal " Stop " in English and German.   This was disregarded, and a warning shot was fired across *Rawalpindi's* bows.   This, too, was disregarded.

About 3.45 the German ship opened fire with her main armament, and *Rawalpindi* replied with her four starboard six-inch guns.   In a very short time the enemy had found the range, and was hitting the British cruiser frequently.   By 4 o'clock the bridge and central controls, the wireless room and the ammunition supply had been blown away.   The ship was on fire fore and aft, and blazing fiercely.   Nevertheless, the guns' crews continued to fire until they, or their guns, had been destroyed.   At least one hit seems to have been registered on the enemy.

The appearance of a second German warship on the port quarter, which opened up a cross-fire, hastened the end.   By a quarter past four every gun had been silenced, and the ship was a blazing mass.

A group of forty to fifty men, and one officer, Lieutenant Pickersgill, gathered on the poop, the only place in the ship not swept by fire.   Some were wounded and in great pain, but no one complained. Without hope of salvation, they shared out their cigarettes and waited quietly for the end.

Suddenly, a waterlogged lifeboat was seen drifting past the ship's side. Most of the men, dazed by the events of the last hour, could not bring themselves to jump thirty feet into the rough sea; but several went over the side, and of these eleven succeeded in climbing into the boat. The blazing pyre of *Rawalpindi* drifted away from them into the night. The next day, numb with cold and utterly exhausted, they were picked up by H.M.S. *Chitral*.

So ended the first naval action of the war. *Rawalpindi* went down with colours flying, and with a grand tradition safe in her keeping. No greater tribute could be paid to her Captain, and the officers and men who manned her, than the simple words of the Prime Minister in the House of Commons four days later. " They must have known as soon as they sighted the enemy that there was no chance for them, but they had no thought of surrender. They fought their guns till they could be fought no more. They then—many of them—went to their deaths, and thereby carried on the great traditions of the Royal Navy. Their example will be an inspiration to those who come after them."

CHAPTER SIX

SHORE TRAINING

I

Some people have jobs in this war which are interesting, exciting and do not call for much personal discomfort. Looking after a barrage balloon is not one of them. During a divisional course at Portsmouth (where I was appointed in January, 1940), I found myself in charge of one for a night in the dockyard.

My first duty was to see that it was firmly bedded down. After surveying its vast body from every angle, and satisfying myself that it was not likely to move far under its own steam, I went to my cabin on board Nelson's flagship, *Victory*, where I was to be accommodated for the night. The chief characteristics of the cabin were a lack of electric light bulbs and a surfeit of beetles.

At about half-past eleven I was awakened by the Leading Seaman in charge, who told me that a Miss Crutch had tripped over one of the wires in the darkness, fallen flat on her face and bashed in most of her teeth. Arrived on the scene, I found Miss Crutch moaning under the shadow of the balloon. I discovered that her injuries amounted to nothing more serious than a cut lip and a bruised elbow, so I despatched her to the sick-bay in the charge of a kindly, three-badge Able Seaman.

It was evident that the wire which had caused Miss Crutch's downfall might, if it were not removed, cause the downfall of others. I ordered it to be shifted to a safe place, and my Leading Seaman superintended the task with agility, and a flow of language which shocked even an old Etonian.

The private soldier's or rating's practice of using bad language indiscriminately is an odd one. Bad language is like vintage port, which should only be taken occasionally, when its value can be appreciated.   Bad language should be reserved for such occasions as falling downstairs, missing the ball or running out of petrol.   If you include it in your everyday speech, how can you express yourself adequately when confronted by a disaster which calls for something stronger than a " Damn " or a " Blast " ?

My Leading Seaman was an able and efficient leading hand, but he would have remained as efficient, I reflected, if he had not prefixed so many of his nouns and verbs by reference to the copulative act.

II

Besides looking after this balloon from time to time (I believe on another occasion it fouled the dockyard railway line, preventing the passage of an ammunition train and delaying the sailing of a battleship for several hours), our duties were many and varied.   We spent a week at the Physical Training School, performing frightful antics on boxes, wall-bars, trapezes and all the other paraphernalia of a gymnasium which most of us had not seen since our private-school days.   The afternoon's exercises started at ten past one, as soon as we had finished lunch, a time of day when the more elderly members of the class had been used to sit comfortably in their club-room armchairs, a glass of port in one hand and a cigar in the other.   During the week's course, two of them broke their ankles ;   the others usually flaked out from exhaustion before the end of the afternoon.

Another week we received instruction at the Signal School. This would sometimes be combined with drill on the parade-ground ;   we would be manœuvred by flag signals made by a specialist signal officer who, for the purpose of the exercise, was the Admiral commanding a flotilla.   We, his destroyers, would march across the parade-ground in columns of three. He might shout the signal which, when hoisted at sea, means " Turn together 180 degrees to starboard "—in other words, " About turn."   At this order, we would raise our right hands above our heads (at sea, ships in company hoist an affirmative flag to show that they have understood the signal) and, on the command " Down " (the hauling down of the Admiral's flag is the executive signal for carrying out the manœuvre), turn smartly about and continue marching in the opposite direction. Of all these signals, the one I liked best was the order for bringing us to a halt. Its literal translation is " Stop Engines."

At Brighton, a variety of entertainment had been at our disposal in the evenings. We might have had an early supper in the mess and visited the Hippodrome ; or we might have spent an hour or two in the big cocktail bar of the Grand before going on to Sweetings for a steak. We might have passed the time in Sherry's dance-hall or the skating-rink, or spent a quiet evening with a friend at the Ship Inn, dining on roast pheasant and a pleasant brand of claret. There were almost endless occupations to choose from.

At Portsmouth, on the other hand, we did one of two things ; we either went to the Queen's or, as I usually did, to bed. The cocktail bar of the Queen's Hotel literally overflowed with naval officers. You could obtain a drink or, if you were lucky, two by pushing hard, and food by pushing harder still.

At ten o'clock the people of Portsmouth call it a day and go to bed. If, however, you feel that the night is young, for half-a-crown you can gain admittance to one of two pseudo night-clubs. Here you can sit back and watch the antics of junior naval officers and Wrens trying to be grown up and pretending that they are enjoying themselves. Both the staff and their customers speak guardedly of the police and of possible raids, liking to believe that they are being naughty, and that the places are dens of iniquity. In point of fact they are puerile, harmless and unexciting. There is something very childish about respectable people trying to be dirty. . . .

A few days before the course was due to end, our Commanding Officer assembled us and broke the news that the special jobs for which we had been trained had been considered impracticable by the Admiralty. He told us that we would have to spend a further period ashore, which was a disappointment. The war had been in progress for nearly five months and all of us were anxious to get to sea. Now we were faced with several more weeks of training at a shore base.

Bill and I walked back to the barracks dejectedly; there, however, we found consolation in a letter from the Admiralty promoting us to be Sub-Lieutenants. With some relief I took my reefer to Gieves the next day to have wavy gold stripes sewn on the cuffs and the hideous red tabs, which had landed me in so many awkward situations, removed from the lapels. Old ladies in buses had mistaken me for the conductor and had offered me pennies. A fatuous Guardee, the peak of whose cap touched the bridge of his nose, had asked me, in a London hotel, whether the lift was going up. I told him that it had broken down, and then had the pleasure of watching him start climbing to his room on the sixth floor. In the same hotel, a pompous business-man had come up to me and asked me point-blank what the red tabs meant.

"Naval Intelligence," I had informed him. "But don't tell a soul!"

He was duly impressed.

III

After Portsmouth came a three-weeks' course at Portland. This was the most interesting of my courses, but because of its confidential nature I cannot describe it—except, perhaps, for a trip in a submarine.

Early one morning I went down to the depot-ship along-side which the submarine flotilla was lying. The officer of the watch ordered me to report on board *H——*, the outside boat of the four. I walked across the wooden gang-planks which connected each submarine with its neighbour, and climbed on board *H——*. There I met the Captain. Two years ago his name was unknown to the public; to-day everybody knows it—Lieutenant-Commander Wanklyn, the first submarine V.C. of the war.*

" 'Morning, Sub," he greeted me. " You're just in time. We're shoving off now."

What seems to impress civilians about the Navy is the calm, confident way in which orders are given and carried out. No shouting, no fuss. They often see the Army at work, especially on the parade-ground, where necessarily there is a great deal of shouting. When they watch the Navy they expect the same thing, and are surprised to discover that there is no noise, because there is no need for it.

I was a civilian then to all intents and purposes, and was deeply impressed by the calm, smooth way in which the Captain poured an almost incessant stream of orders down the voicepipe as we were casting off.

" Let go the headrope—slow ahead starboard—let go aft—half-astern port—port thirty—stop both—midships—starboard twenty—half ahead together."

The boat slid across the calm surface of the harbour and, passing through the boom, pointed its snout to the open sea.

Sitting at a wardroom table, eating pork pies and baked beans sixty feet beneath the surface of the sea, is not, as might be supposed, an odd sensation ; apart from the fact that a submarine has no windows, I might have been sitting in the dining-room at home. So-called observers, who go out for a day's exercise in a submarine and later describe their experiences in the Sunday papers, seem to let their imaginations run away with them.

The exercises began after lunch. From far away we could hear the throb of the engines of vessels hunting us. Ten minutes, a quarter of an hour, twenty minutes passed. Then, scenting our presence like a dog nosing a pheasant out of a hedge, they drew nearer. We heard the even beat of a ship's propellers directly overhead ; it sounded like an express train going through a tunnel.

* Since writing this, the junior officer of *H*——, Lieutenant Peter Roberts, has also been awarded the V.C.

By three o'clock the exercises were completed, and the Captain ordered stations for surfacing. Each man stood by his instrument, quickly and efficiently carrying out the orders which concerned him. Wheels were turned, levers pulled, switches made. I felt her tilt slightly as the tanks were blown ; then we nosed our way slowly to the surface.

The journey back to harbour was uneventful. We passed through the boom shortly before five o'clock and proceeded across the harbour at half-speed towards the depot-ship. The same swift, smooth orders from the Captain : " Half-astern starboard—starboard twenty—stop starboard—midships—slow astern together—stop both—haul taut and belay—ring off main engines." The wires were secured and doubled up, the gang-plank was placed in position and the Captain went ashore. The submarine was made fast for the night.

CHAPTER SEVEN

NEW BOY

I

On the 9th March, 1940, I sat in a first-class compartment of the Scottish express, watching the countryside slip by and trying to form some picture of the new world I was about to enter. My appointment to a sea-going ship had come through at last. The long months of training were over, and I was heading for a "northern port" where, according to the instructions on the slip of paper in my breast pocket, I was to report for duty on board H.M.S. *T——*. I could not have hoped for a better appointment ; before leaving London, I had learnt that *T——* was one of the most modern and powerful destroyers attached to the Home Fleet. If any ship was likely to see action, it was she.

Towards evening the train drew into the seaport station. A taxi brought me to the Navy offices on the front, where I enquired for my ship. No one knew anything about her. After questioning an Able Seaman, a Chief Petty Officer and a Paymaster Sub-Lieutenant, none of whom could throw any light on *T——'s* whereabouts, I got exasperated.

"She must be here," I complained. "Look, it says so on this piece of paper." I produced my appointment from the Admiralty.

The Paymaster Sub-Lieutenant laughed. "That doesn't mean a thing," he said. "Why, only yesterday we had an officer here who'd been to five different ports in the past three weeks trying to catch up with his ship."

"Did he find her all right yesterday?" I asked.

"No, she'd sailed the day before for Southampton. Bit of bad luck, wasn't it? But I'll go and ask the Captain's secretary about you. He may know something."

The Captain's secretary knew something, thank heaven.

T—— had sailed only a few hours before, but was not expected to be long at sea. Until she returned, I was to be accommodated in *W*——.

W—— was an immense, frightening-looking battleship at anchor in the bay. I was taken aboard her late that evening in a fast picket-boat.

I was lost in that battleship, metaphorically and literally. I recollect being led to the wardroom, where I was given whiskies and sodas, and then being whisked off by a marine, who led me in almost total darkness up ladders, along passages, down ladders, until we came to rest outside a cabin marked " Captain of the Fleet."

" Who," I wondered, as I came to a halt behind the marine, " is the Captain of the Fleet, and what in the name of God does he want with me at this hour of the night ? "

The marine had no such inhibitions ; without knocking, he turned the handle, threw open the door and switched on the light. I saw a large cabin, empty except for two chests of drawers and three camp-beds. Tufts of hair on the pillows of two of them indicated that they were already occupied ; the remaining bed, I guessed, was for me.

" There you are, sir," said the marine, " and I 'ope you'll be comfortable. Good-night, sir."

Next morning I was awakened by my companions, two burly Engineer Sub-Lieutenants, who told me that if I wanted breakfast I had better " shake a leg." The table was cleared at a quarter to nine punctually, and it was now twenty-five to. I dressed, quickly and inadequately, and set out in the direction of the gunroom. I had not got far before I realised that I was lost again. A three-badge Able Seaman came to my rescue.

" Gunroom is it you want, sorr ? " said this Irishman. " You are the wrong end of the ship altogether." He led me up a ladder on to the upper deck, thence on to the quarterdeck, and down another ladder to the door of the gunroom.

" My name is Kelly, sorr," he said, " and if you're wanting assistance any other time, I'll be glad to give it to you. I have been in the service twenty-three years."

7

The inmates of the gunroom were a dozen midshipmen and six sub-lieutenants ; I was to live in their company for the next three days, as bewildered by their conversation as by the geography of the ship.   They seldom discussed anything but " shop " ; personalities and parts of the ship were referred to by initials.   There were the A.D.P., the S.O.O., the E.A., the S.D.O., the P.M.O., the D.C.T., and many others.   There were references to " bricks," " fish," " gash," " guff," " kettles," " whizzers," and " the heads," which I soon discovered meant the lavatory.   There was a rating called " the Buffer," and another known as the " Chief G.I."   The Captain was referred to as " The Master," " The Owner " or, more familiarly, " Father."   Each officer had his nickname according to his station.   The First Lieutenant was " Number One," the Signal Officer " Flags," the Dentist " Toothie," and so on.   By the end of three days, I had memorised some useful phrases.

When *T——* returned to harbour I packed my few belongings, said good-bye to my hosts and to Able Seaman Kelly, whom I happened to pass on the quarterdeck, and climbed down the gangway into the boat.   I saw my ship for the first time lying alongside an oiler.   She was a fine-looking vessel, with sloping bows and gracious lines.   Her main armament of 4·7-inch guns stood out boldly against the evening sky ; the White Ensign fluttered at her mainmast. I thanked God then that I had not been appointed to a drifter or a trawler as many of my messmates at *King Alfred* and Portsmouth had been.   Here was a ship built to attack. Here were power and majesty and beauty ; sleek, sharp lines and wicked-looking guns ; bows which could cut through the water like scissors through paper ; a streamlined bridge from which to command, and to control the power of forty-four thousand horse.   Amidships were the tubes housing the " tin fish," those sinister weapons which speed through the water at forty knots and approach their target unseen, and often unheard.

As we approached the ship I tried to remember the advice

the C.O. at Portsmouth had given me. " When you join your ship for the first time," he had said, " salute the officer of the watch smartly and say ' Come aboard to join, sir.' Remember, it's first impressions which count."

The midshipman of the picket-boat brought his craft alongside *T*——'s stern. The bowman grabbed the guard-rail with his boathook, the stern-sheetman did the same. There was no gangway, so I clambered on to the quarterdeck, my luggage following. The picket-boat shoved off.

From my pile of luggage I looked around me. The upper deck was deserted. It was rather an anticlimax.

I made my way to the Engineer's Bridge amidships, where I came across a stoker sitting on an upturned N.A.A.F.I. crate, chewing gum.

" Where would I find the officer of the watch ? " I asked him. He replied :

" Ain't no officer of the watch aboard 'ere, sir, leastways not in 'arbour." He let this statement sink in, so that I could contemplate my ignorance, then continued :

" The officer *you* want to see is the officer of the day, sir, and if I'm not mistaken, you'll find him partaking of his evening gin in the wardroom." He added as an afterthought, " Only find officers of the watch in harbour in big ships, you know, sir."

I returned aft, and was going to start a search for the ward-room when a figure, whose monkey-jacket bore two gold stripes, bounded out of the after lobby.

" Glad to see you, old boy," said the Lieutenant. " Sorry I wasn't here to welcome you before. Come on down and have a drink."

I followed him down the steep iron ladder to the wardroom, where I met my fellow officers for the first time : the Captain —a Commander, whose seamanship and language on the bridge were to receive my admiration (this was his seventh command); the First Lieutenant, who was soon leaving to assume his own command ; Henry, the Number 2, who had welcomed me, an ex-R.N.R. Officer ; Tiny, the R.N.V.R. Lieutenant, a mass of flesh and bone (six months before he had been stockbroking in the City); Spider, the navigating officer, a brilliant and efficient Sub-Lieutenant R.N.; the Doctor, who had recently qualified at Edinburgh University; the Chief, the Flotilla Schoolmaster and the Gunner.

Before I had been in the ship a day I realised my ignorance. During training ashore I had been taught technical stuff. I knew how the A/S gear worked, how to fire a torpedo and to apply deflection; I knew a little about navigation, pilotage and gunnery. But about the organisation and daily routine of a man-of-war I knew nothing. The little I had picked up during my three days in *W*—— helped me considerably. But there was one word, used by everybody, which baffled me for a long time. It was *Pusser*. There were Pusser's soap, Pusser's peas, Pusser's pants, Pusser's boats and Pusser's tobacco. I approached the Sub (who never spared himself to explain something new to me) and asked him who Pusser was.

He was amused at my ignorance. When he had stopped laughing he told me, " Pusser's short for Paymaster. Pusser's stores are naval stores."

That incident happened nearly two years ago, but I haven't heard the last of it yet.

Another time, a few weeks later, when I was officer of the day, the Captain sent for me and said, " Kennedy, what's the cat doing? Someone's moved it."

It struck me as odd that the captain of a two-thousand-ton destroyer should, at that particular moment, be interested in the ship's cat, but it was not my business to question it. The captain of one of H.M. ships is an uncrowned king. If he wants to know how the ship's cat is spending the afternoon he must be told.

I came out of the after lobby on to the quarterdeck, where the quartermaster was keeping his watch. He hadn't seen the cat, nor had the bosun's mate whom I met in the canteen flat on my way forward. In fact, no one had seen the cat.

I started searching for it. I searched the after flat, the

wardroom flat and the after lobby. I whistled and shouted for it. I looked for it under the First Lieutenant's bunk (one of its favourite haunts) but only succeeded in waking the First Lieutenant from his afternoon "zizz," which didn't please him. I looked for it in the galley and in the heads. In fact I looked everywhere, and eventually ran it to earth on X Gun Deck, curled up on a coil of rope.

I returned to the Captain's cabin.

" Er, about the cat, Sir."

" Oh yes, Kennedy. You've been the devil of a time. Well, what's happened to it ? "

" It's asleep on a coil of rope on X Gun Deck, Sir."

For a moment I thought the Captain was going to contravene King's Regulations and Admiralty Instructions by doing me violence. His eyes bulged, his cheeks took on a purplish tinge and he banged the table with his fist.

" No, no, you bloody fool," he said, " not the cat, the *catamaran*. Somebody's moved it. B——r the cat ! "

I left quietly and confided my trouble to the Sub, who told me, between bursts of laughter, that the catamaran was the raft which separated us from the capital ship we were lying alongside. Later, I looked up the word in a dictionary ; it was defined as " a raft used by the natives of Madras to paddle from one village to another." But I never told that to the Captain.

II

The day after I joined *T*—— sailed again. I did not know where we were going, nor had I the courage to ask ; but when I came up on to the bridge for my first watch at four o'clock the next morning I saw a coastline which I recognised —Islay. Above the summits of its hills towered the Paps of Jura, their snow-capped peaks ranging each brae and burn from Sgurr na Ghillean to Goat Fell. Nearer, I could make out the shadowy shapes of the Rhinns of Islay through the inshore mist. As we drew closer, the Portnahaven lighthouse came into sight and, as the mists rolled away with the morning light, the farm at Cladville where my father and I had spent such happy days the previous summer. Through my binoculars I recognised familiar landmarks—the barn on the hillside where we used to picnic, a long low wall behind which we used to wait for the evening flight of pigeon, a boggy patch of land called " the marsh," which abounded in snipe, and, to seaward, the bare, rugged cliffs on whose crests we had waited many hours for duck, pigeon and plover.

I sipped the cup of cocoa the bosun's mate had handed me and watched the hills of Islay until they, and the memories they held, vanished into the mists.

CHAPTER EIGHT

WARDROOM

I

They will tell you at the Admiralty that this is a destroyers' war. That is not to say that the battleships, cruisers, submarines, minesweepers and auxiliary units of the Navy are not doing magnificent work. But battleships are built to fight other battleships ; cruisers, because of their powers of endurance, to carry out long patrols ; submarines for their patrols ; minesweepers to keep the coastal channels clear for traffic. Destroyers are maids of all work. Their size, speed, endurance and fighting power have fitted them for escorting convoys, hunting U-Boats, screening the Battle Fleet, assisting damaged ships, raiding the enemy's coastline, and many other jobs besides.

The minesweepers, anti-submarine craft and other smaller vessels of the Fleet must all face hardship and rough weather ; but their patrols are fixed, and they can look forward to a night in harbour from time to time and be sure of getting it. Not the destroyers, which must be ready to proceed to sea at any hour of the day or night. A U-Boat has been reported fifty miles away and must be hunted, a torpedoed merchant ship needs assistance, or perhaps a German raider has left port and the battleships must be escorted to sea in search of it. Many destroyers which took part in the operations off Norway in the Spring of 1941 were at sea for twenty-five or twenty-six days a month during that campaign.

But life in a destroyer is not altogether a tough one. Ask any officer or rating whether he would exchange his ship for a cruiser or battleship, and ninety-nine times out of a hundred he will answer " Not likely ! " It is true that the living quarters are cramped, there are few facilities for recreation, in a rough sea the mess-decks are often flooded, and at speed the motion is uncomfortable. Apart from these inconveniences, the advantages are tremendous.

In a big ship you are one cog in a vast piece of machinery; you know some of your fellow cogs, but not all of them. In a destroyer you each have your responsibilities, and very heavy some of them are. Driving two thousand tons of steel, containing two hundred of your fellow men, through the water at twenty-five knots on a dark night is a job which calls for every minute of your attention. There are seldom more than a dozen officers in a destroyer, and you get to know them intimately. The Captain, unlike his aloof and seldom-seen counterpart in a big ship, lives mostly in the wardroom. When the ship puts to sea he will probably tell you where she is going and how long she will be out. In a big ship only a handful of officers, besides the Pussers who do the cyphers (and whose lips are sealed), know something, or anything, of her future movements.

The difference between living in a battleship and living in a destroyer is the difference between living at the Ritz and at the Pig and Whistle. If you like the Ritz, go to a battleship. I prefer the Pig and Whistle.

At sea, the bridge of a modern destroyer is the control centre of the ship. In the centre of it is a raised daïs known as the compass platform, in the middle of which stands the pelorus, which houses the compass. From behind this the officer of the watch controls the movements of the ship. A voicepipe on the right of the pelorus communicates with the quartermaster at the wheel below; one on the left communicates with the Captain's sea-cabin.

The bridge abounds in telephones and instruments. There are telephones to the engine-room, the quarterdeck, the Director Control Tower, the close-range armament, the after control, the torpedo-tubes—in fact to every key position in the ship. There are voicepipes to the gyro-compass room, the crow's-nest, the anti-submarine cabinet, the wireless office, the signal distributing office, the flag-deck and the charthouse. In the front of the bridge is the famous Asdic gear, by which so many U-Boats have been destroyed.   A clock-like dial on the left is the automatic log, and a recess in front of the pelorus the chart-table.

At the back of the bridge, and above it, stands the Director Control Tower.   It is a circular steel structure, mounted on a revolving pedestal, from which the Gunnery Control Officer controls the main armament.   He trains the D.C.T. on to the target and the guns follow round on to the same bearing. He passes his orders down a voicepipe to the Transmitting Station, a small cabinet in the heart of the ship where the calculations for deflection and elevation are worked out automatically on instruments and passed on to the guns.

Naval gunnery is a complex business.   Not only must the speed and direction of the wind be taken into consideration, but also ballistic errors, and other factors unimportant to a land gunner.   Allowances must be made for your own and the enemy's speed, his inclination towards or away from you, the rate at which you are closing him, the angle at which you will get all your guns to bear on him, and other technicalities which, if overlooked, may make the difference between a hit and a miss.   The tactical situation is changing literally from second to second; the calculations are worked out by mathematics and trigonometry, which the astonishing instruments in the Transmitting Station solve automatically.

During the four hours he is on duty, the officer of the watch, as the Captain's representative, is in command of the ship.   He must report to the Captain everything which happens on the bridge—all ships and aircraft encountered, land sighted, and any matter which might affect the safety of the ship.   But his primary duty is to steer the course which the navigator has given him or, if in company with the Fleet, which the flagship has ordered.

If the ship is in company, the officer of the watch must keep correct bearing and distance on the senior officer—a devilish hard job until you have got the hang of it.   Say, for instance, you are stationed on the port bow of the flagship, which bears 140°, 2,000 yards away, on a course of 360°, or due north.

8

Your attention is diverted momentarily by the approach of an aeroplane and, when you look at the compass again, you find that the flagship bears 132°, 2,200 yards distant. In this case it is a simple matter to correct yourself. You lay the centre of your azimuth along a line of bearing of 140°, and see that the line of bearing is astern of the flagship. You are therefore astern of station; but you are still ahead of the ship you are screening, so that by steering in (that is, to starboard) you can adjust your bearing and, at the same time, decrease the range.

You are now in station again. But say, when you look at the compass a little later, the bearing has returned to 132°, while the range is only 1,800 yards. Steering in will decrease the range further; you must increase speed by a few revolutions and thus get back to your original line of bearing, at the same time, by drawing away, increasing the range. A good officer of the watch, they say, has no need to alter speed to adjust his station.

A kind-hearted Admiral will tolerate inefficient station-keeping for perhaps a quarter of an hour; then he will order his signal officer to hoist the pendants of the defaulting ship, followed by the flags which mean " H.M.S. —— take up appointed station! " If the matter is not then rectified, he will call for the name of the officer of the watch, which will be hoisted ignominiously at the masthead for the whole fleet to see.

Beside the officer of the watch stands the yeoman or signalman of the watch, and in each corner of the bridge is a look-out. Each look-out has a sector of 90° (from the beam to right ahead or astern) which he is supposed to sweep continuously with his glasses; but more often it is the officer of the watch or the signalman who sights an object first. You might think that the officer of the watch has his hands full, but that depends on the position and intentions of the ship. In coastal waters he must be on the top line every minute of his watch and check up on his position frequently by taking bearings of lighthouses, and by echo-sounding—at the same time keeping a constant look-out for the approach of enemy air or surface craft. But often, far out in the Atlantic, the hours drag by heavily. He looks at the compass occasionally to see that the quartermaster is on the right course, or searches the sea with his glasses for a lurking periscope. Apart from that there is little to relieve the monotony. Cigarettes and cups of cocoa follow each other in an unbroken chain until the minute-hand of the Admiralty clock has coincided with the hour-hand for the fourth and last time.

The Captain appears on the bridge only occasionally. For the most part he remains in his sea-cabin below it, a bored and often lonely man, so that when the time comes for his ship to hoist the battle-ensign and clear for action he will be able to stay " up top " indefinitely. His life in war-time is by no means easy. He alone bears the responsibility for the safety of his ship, and must be kept informed of everything, literally everything, which takes place on the bridge. Say, for instance, that course is altered two or three times during the night and, towards dawn, various shore lights are observed. That means that the Captain must be called half a dozen times during the night, and must rouse himself sufficiently to digest each piece of information and retain it in his brain, so that when he decides to go on to the bridge he will have a clear picture of what has been happening. Add to this the tension of navigating at night in coastal waters (where there are few aids to navigation these days), and of going alongside oilers in the dark, and you will have an idea of the nervous strain imposed upon him. Of course, he will receive the first laurels if the ship comes out of battle gloriously ; but if, on the other hand, when attacking a U-Boat the depth charges fail to explode through negligent handling (actually the responsibility of the Gunner (T)), the Captain will be the first to feel the weight of " their Lordship's displeasure."

II

In harbour the routine is slightly different; regular watches are kept only by the engine-room and communication departments, and the quarterdeck staff. The bosun's mate calls the hands at six in the morning, piping " All the hands ! Heave-ho, heave-ho ! Lash up and stow ! " When the hammocks have been taken down and stowed, the hands are piped to breakfast. After that, the morning's work begins.

It may be painting ship, cleaning guns or whatever the First Lieutenant orders. The First Lieutenant is second in command of the ship; on his shoulders falls the responsibility of seeing that she is run smoothly and efficiently in harbour. A good First Lieutenant will instil the right spirit and confidence in the ship's company so that he can get the best out of them. Then he will be certain that the ship will not only look smart, but also be in the first condition of fighting efficiency.

At eight o'clock the colours are hoisted at the mainmast; while this ceremony is in progress everyone on the upper deck must come to attention and face aft. The officer of the day salutes the colours from the quarterdeck and, when the ensign has been run up to the masthead, orders the bosun's mate to pipe the " carry on."

The officer of the day, like the officer of the watch at sea, is responsible for the safety of the ship in harbour, and is on duty from nine o'clock one morning until nine o'clock the next. He has to superintend (under the orders of the First Lieutenant) the lowering, running and hoisting of the ship's boats (which, in most destroyers, do not seem capable of working for more than about two hours on end), calling out the duty part of the watch to take in stores or secure another ship alongside, and so on. He must have a thorough knowledge of what is happening from hour to hour. He must inspect the libertymen before they go ashore and when they come back : before, to satisfy himself that they are clean, smart and a credit to the ship ; after, to make sure that bottles of beer are not lurking in trouser pockets. He must receive guests, pipe the Captain over the side and, at midnight, go the rounds before turning in.

Interviewing defaulters is another of his duties. Suppose that Able Seaman Snooks, in a fit of rage, has called Petty Officer Snodgrass, his superior officer, a b——y s——d. Petty Officer Snodgrass reports the matter to the petty officer of the day, who orders Able Seaman Snooks to fall in on the quarterdeck before the officer of the day. When the latter, who has probably been enjoying a quiet " zizz " in the wardroom, appears a conversation such as this takes place :

P.O.O.D. (To Snooks) : " Atten*shun* ! Off caps ! "

Snooks, looking a bit sheepish, removes his cap with his right hand.

P.O.O.D. (To O.O.D., saluting) : " Able Seaman Snooks, sir. Did make use of improper language to Petty Officer Snodgrass, his superior officer."

O.O.D. (To Snodgrass) : " What do you know about this ? "

Snodgrass (all in one breath) : " It was like this, sir. I was standing outside the galley, superintending the lowering of the whaler, when I sees Able Seaman Snooks, who is in the whaler's crew, slouching out of the flat ; so I asks him why he is late, and he says I never heard the pipe. Rubbish, I says to him, everyone else has heard it ; now get on your life-belt and get into that whaler double quick time. He then uses improper language to me."

O.O.D. : " What were the exact words he used ? "

Snodgrass : " He called me a b——y s——d, sir ! "

O.O.D. " Right, that's all, thank you. Now then, Snooks, you've heard what Petty Officer Snodgrass has to say. Is this true ? "

In his defence, Snooks will repeat the story Snodgrass has told, but will omit any reference to swearing. The officer of the day will ask him : " Did you call Petty Officer Snodgrass a b——y s——d ? "

The answer will be either, " Not in a manner of speaking "

if Snooks thinks he has a chance of getting away with it, or
" in a manner of speaking, yes " if he considers that there is too
much evidence against him.

When the evidence has been heard, the officer of the day
will say " Case dismissed " or, more often, " First Lieutenant's
report." If the defaulter is put on the First Lieutenant's
report the story must be retold at the " Requestmen and
Defaulters' Table " which the First Lieutenant holds twice a
week. The First Lieutenant may punish the man himself or,
if the charge is serious, pass it on to the Captain's report, when
the story must be told a third time.

The Captain can award a number of punishments. He can
give a man so many days No. 11 or No. 16 (a scale of extra
work laid down in King's Regulations), deprive him of a
good-conduct badge, stop his pay and his leave, or even send
him to prison.

Not long ago I was hearing the evidence in a very serious
case. Two of the most senior ratings in the ship were
enemies. Living together in the same small mess for four
months at sea proved too much for them, and one morning
they came to blows. The damage was considerable; most
of the lights in the mess were smashed, one rating had his
head cut open, but had himself broken three of the other's
ribs. Because the case was serious, I was taking down the
evidence in writing.

Smith was describing the battle :

" Brown calls me a dirty bastard, sir, so I takes off my
coat and I goes to haction stations. During the engage-
ment—— "

" All right," I said; " not so fast, please. Remember, I've
got to take all this down."

I scribbled for a few seconds, then my pencil broke. I
stopped writing and tried to let through more lead.

Smith thought I had stuck.

" Only one ' s ' in bastard, sir," he said.

III

Although the chief duty of an executive officer is watch-keeping, his work is by no means finished when the ship returns to harbour. One of the busiest officers in harbour is the correspondence officer, who is in charge of the official mail.

In big ships this job is carried out by Pussers assisted by Writers. As there are no Pussers in destroyers, it is usually taken on by a Sub R.N.V.R. He and his Writer work in a small office known as the Ship's Office, where he keeps the pay for the ship's company, the service certificates (known as " stiff tickets," because they are written on parchment) of ratings borne on the ship's books, orders and instructions issued by the Admiralty and Flag Officers, and a record of correspondence between the Commanding Officer and outside authorities. All incoming correspondence is addressed to the Commanding Officer, whether it concerns the conduct of the ship in action or the decrease in the allotment Ordinary Seaman Smith makes to his mother.

Destroyers are organised in flotillas, each flotilla consisting of eight ships, of which one is the leader; her captain is known as Captain (Destroyers), or Captain (D) for short. Captain (D) is a four-ringed Captain (" private " destroyers are commanded by Commanders or Lieutenant-Commanders), and he and his staff—qualified specialist officers of Lieutenant's rank or above—attend to the needs of the destroyers in the flotilla. Captain (D) is the destroyers' Administrative Authority, and a copy of any letter concerning the administration of the ship is sent to him.

A number of destroyer flotillas constitutes a squadron, which is administered by an officer of Flag Rank, known as Rear-Admiral (D), or R.A. (D) for short. It is safe to say that seventy-five per cent of a destroyer's official mail is addressed to R.A. (D) or Captain (D).

In a destroyer which my present Captain commanded a few

years ago the correspondence officer, a Sub-Lieutenant R.N., was unfortunately washed overboard and drowned. On returning to harbour the Captain went down to the Ship's Office to straighten out the correspondence. Instead of the usual clutter found in the Ship's Office of a destroyer he was surprised to see that the files were practically empty and the desk clear of papers except for three bulky packets. The first was labelled " Tripe from R.A. (D)," the second " Tripe from Captain (D)," and the third " Miscellaneous Tripe."

Cruisers and ships of higher tonnage carry their own accounts ; those of destroyers are kept in the destroyer depot-ship. Every other Friday the correspondence officer calls on the squadron accountant officer in the depot-ship to collect the fortnightly pay-list and pay, amounting to several hundred pounds. The money supplied is usually in excess of the amount required ; Jones has been discharged to hospital, or Brown and Robinson have left the ship. The correspondence officer takes this on charge in his contingent account, of which he must keep a balance-sheet. Other moneys which pass through the contingent account are the proceeds from the sale of Pusser's tobacco and soap, pension payments, payments for travelling expenses, a sum claimed by the postman each month for official postage, and casual payments. The monthly turnover is eight to nine hundred pounds.

The responsibility of keeping a true statement of the contingent account has caused the hair of many young officers to turn grey. I have been spared anxiety myself because I have always made it a rule to balance the cash after each payment ; and of an odd £20,000 which passed through my hands during eighteen months, I can honestly say that I mislaid only a few shillings. Matters might have been different if I had followed the advice of my predecessor, a slapdash fellow who, when he turned over the keys of the safe, gave me this warning. " When you tot up your balance at the end of the month you will find that you have twenty-three pounds five shillings and ninepence more than you

5 THE SHIP'S COMPANY OF H.M.S. *T——*

6 SPIDER   7 THE CAPTAIN

8, 9 LOOKING FORWARD AND AFT FROM THE CROW'S NEST

ought to have. The second time you add it up you will find that you ought to have seven pounds and a penny more than you actually have. When you add it up the third time you will be one to two pounds up or down. Don't bother to add it up again ; that's the correct answer ! "

In harbour, the navigation officer keeps the corrections to his charts up to date, the signal officer amends the numerous signal publications every ship carries, and the C.B. officer checks his confidential books. The Gunner (T) inspects his torpedoes and checks over the ammunition of which he is in charge, and the Chief divides his day between making the motor-boat work and supervising the alterations and additions which are to be carried out at the next refit. Only the Doctor, whose work for the day finishes after his surgery at nine o'clock each morning, finds that time hangs heavily on his hands. Recently qualified and keen to play his part in the life of the ship, he discovers that his work for the day consists in prescribing medicine for half a dozen coughs and examining a few suspected cases of scabies. But he knows, as all of us know, that the day the ship hoists her battle-ensign and steams into action his services will be priceless. Until that day, he must be content to twiddle his thumbs and order another gin.

CHAPTER NINE

NORWAY

I

I didn't have to wait long for my first taste of excitement.

One evening, soon after I had joined, we were entering harbour after a rather exhausting six days at sea. I was in the wardroom playing double cameroons with the Doc, Tiny and Henry, with whom I was discussing the prospects of getting shore leave to visit the nearest big town. Suddenly the duty signalman came in. Henry took the pad, and I could tell by the way his brows puckered that the news was bad.

" It's from the C.-in-C.," he said. " We're to prepare to leave immediately after oiling."

" Another ruddy middle," said Tiny. " Christ! And I thought I'd got a night in."

" Good show ! " said Henry. " I've got the day. Nothing for me now until the forenoon."

" Wonder what the flap is this time," said Number One, and went up to the bridge to find out.

We didn't have to wait long to hear what the flap was. That night, as we formed up in line ahead and steamed out of harbour, we learnt that the Germans had invaded Norway, and that a large part of their fleet was at sea. . . .

The scene when I came on watch the next morning was impressive. We had joined the rest of the Fleet ; ahead and on either beam were destroyers—line upon line of destroyers, each keeping perfect station on its next ahead. Astern of us was the main body of the Fleet, battleships, cruisers and an aircraft carrier. Flanking the Fleet on either hand, but stationed six or seven miles away, were the scouting cruisers, ready to give warning of the approach of the enemy.

We steamed southwards during the forenoon, hoping to locate and engage the main German Fleet ; but we saw nothing except an increasing number of mines—black, bulbous brutes which only showed themselves for a moment when thrown on to the crest of a wave. We had to take avoiding action continuously, and there was seldom a period when at least one destroyer was not flying the signal " Mine starboard or port."

Just before I came off watch at twelve-thirty the Commander-in-Chief ordered a turn of 180 degrees. It was a wonderful sight to watch the leaders of each column swing round together to starboard when the executive signal was hauled down, the destroyers astern following in succession in their wake. To an inexperienced officer this would have been a tricky manœuvre, but to the Captain it was child's-play. He stood behind the pelorus, his keen eyes watching every movement of the ship ahead, not uttering a sound until the bow of the ship began to draw away from the wake ahead. Then: " Port twenty—twenty-five—ease to fifteen—midships—port ten—ease and follow." We passed the flagship on opposite courses. When we were approaching our new station the battleships turned, so that when they had steadied on the new course it needed only a few adjustments to the revolutions to regain correct station.

That afternoon we were detached, in company with three Polish destroyers, to proceed to a point on the Norwegian coast to escort to England a big convoy which had so far escaped the enemy's attention. The Poles formed up in quarter-line on our port quarter, and we set course for the North-East. The friendly shapes of the Fleet disappeared slowly from sight.

We might run into anything now. We knew that a German destroyer flotilla had reached Narvik, but beyond that, and the news that several of their warships had entered Oslo Harbour, no one was sure where the main body of their forces was.

I turned in during the afternoon, to be awakened by the shrill peal of the alarm bells. I leapt out of my bunk, snatched my steel helmet and glasses from the peg and went up to my action station at Y Gun. The supply party switched on the electric motor to the ammunition supply hoist, and a moment later I heard the throbbing whine of the gun pumps as the engine-room applied pressure. The trainer followed round his pointer to the maximum forward bearing, and we waited.

For a time I could see nothing, as my view was obscured by the flag-deck and the Carley floats on the fo'c'sle. Then I caught a glimpse of a dull grey object about seven miles away, and wondered what we were up against. If it were a destroyer, the four of us could annihilate her quite easily; if it were a cruiser, we would probably score one or two torpedo hits, but would have to face up to a terrific plastering before we got within range. Luckily, the ship turned out to be a Swedish merchantman making for home and, in view of recent events, keeping a healthy distance from the coast. She passed within five cables of us, dipping her ensign in salute.

We met the convoy that evening—thirty or forty ships strung out to seaward from the coast in a long, wavering line. When we got within signalling distance, one of the ships made to us, " Two German merchantmen have been observed steaming up —— Fjord." A glance at the chart told the Captain that —— Fjord was only a few miles to northward, and he debated whether to detach one of the Poles to intercept them. The temptation must have been great, as it was the kind of job the Poles were waiting for. However, we formed up the convoy in four columns as night fell, and began the long journey home. Next morning, a shadowing aircraft made a brief appearance about twenty thousand feet overhead. We stood by for a bombing attack in the afternoon, but none came. Evidently the Hun was too busy elsewhere.

After that the trip was uneventful. We reached England three days later in quicker time than had been made by any convoy on the route, which was not surprising, as every ship was anxious to get as far from the Norwegian coast as possible, as quickly as possible. The masters handled their vessels magnificently; nearly all of them answered our flag signals, and the leaders of the columns even repeated them. We made several tricky turns during the night, expecting to find next morning that some ships had got lost or had turned the wrong way. The convoy system was still in its early stages then, and that sort of thing often happened.

But for three days each ship kept its position in the line. The day before we reached England there was one straggler, a little thousand-ton Norwegian ship which Spider christened " Runt." When she had dropped a mile and a half astern we made a wide circle and approached to within four cables, flying the signal " Increase speed." This had no effect, so Spider got out a blackboard from the signal distributing office. On this he wrote " GO FASTER " in big letters, and slung the notice over the side of the bridge. As this met with the same result, the Captain took the ship within a cable of " Runt " and, picking up his megaphone, bellowed " Can't you go any faster ? "

Nothing happened for a few minutes. Then a figure appeared in the wings of " Runt's " bridge and, cupping his hands to his mouth, shouted in broken English, " I go slow."

" Yes, I know that," answered the Captain, " but go faster, can't you ? "

" I go slow," the voice repeated. " My engine goes slow."

We gave it up then, and headed back to our position on the port bow. We had hardly reached it when clouds of black smoke began to pour out of " Runt's " funnel ; an aeroplane thirty miles away could have spotted us. We raced back towards her.

" Stop that smoke ! " bellowed the Captain through his megaphone.

" I go fast now," came the reply. " My engine goes fast."

That was true. Within a very short time " Runt " had caught up with the convoy and regained her position in the line. The black smoke ceased as suddenly as it had begun.

Next day, in perfect sunshine and on a calm sea, we entered harbour. The Poles formed astern of us in line ahead to pass through the boom. As we steamed down the line of merchant ships they hoisted the signal " Thank you for your escort."

" Thank you.   Good luck ! " the Captain replied.

II

For the next two months we were at sea almost continuously, only entering harbour to oil and provision before leaving again.   Luckily the weather held, otherwise we would have got considerably more bolo than we did.   Shore leave was out of the question, and the only thing to which we really looked forward was the mail.   The authorities were very good in seeing that we got it regularly.   Once, after we had been at sea for some time, our flotilla leader passed it over on a line. I was on watch at the time, and the steward brought my letters up with the forenoon soup at eleven.   It seemed odd to be reading a letter from home in the middle of the North Sea. . . .

The Germans had complete command of the air in Norway. The other destroyers were bombed severely, but although we saw a great many aircraft, none attacked us.   " Lucky *T*——" we were called in the flotilla.

As the days passed, it became clear that our forces in Norway were losing ground under heavy, persistent air attacks, aided by fifth-column activity ; so we were not surprised to be ordered to proceed, in company with the transport *U*——, to evacuate British forces at M——.   I had known M—— in peacetime ; it was one of those charming little places to be found up and down the fjords of Western Norway.   My parents and I had called in there one evening many years before in a small Norwegian coasting steamer, the *Sigurd Jarl*, on our way to Trondheim.   I remembered it as one of the most beautiful and peaceful places I had ever visited.

We went to action stations some time before the coast of Norway came in sight and, at dusk, approached the entrance to the fjord up which M—— lay.   It had been a day of

glorious sunshine, the sea as flat as a billiard-table. The
mountains towered above us on either hand, rising out of a
low sea mist, and the setting sun traced patterns of gold and
silver on their snowy summits. We steamed slowly up the
fjord, keeping a sharp watch for aircraft swooping down
from behind the hills; and I thought of the last time I had
steamed up that fjord sitting on the deck of the *Sigurd Jarl*,
listening contentedly to a Norwegian merchant playing *Den
Norske Fiskerman* and other Norwegian folk-songs on a
portable gramophone.

We were not far up the fjord when one of the supply party
stewards exclaimed, " Cor —— me ! Take a look at that,
Lofty ! " Ahead of us, still a long way away, a dull, red glow
suffused the sky. It deepened and spread as we approached,
and we saw tongues of flame shooting above the treetops.
Then, rounding a bend in the fjord, I saw the town of M——.
Not a house had escaped the German bombers; every building was either in flames or so gutted that there was nothing
left to burn. We made fast along the jetty, the *U*—— a cable
ahead of us. A gangway was put ashore amidships, just clear
of a huge bomb-crater, and Number One went ashore to get
in touch with the naval officer in charge.

I paced the upper deck, keeping an eye on the gangway.
Most of the sailors wanted to go ashore for a goof (" just a
quick look rahnd, sir "), and I had my hands full stopping
them. " Guns " took photographs from the quarterdeck;
otherwise we remained at action stations.

I saw a figure walking along the jetty dressed in the resplen-
dent uniform of a Norwegian colonel. He came over the
gangway, and I saluted him as he stepped on board.

" I wish to see the General," he said. " Where is he ? "

" Do you mean the Captain ? " I asked him.

" Yes. I wish to see him. Where is he ? "

I took him down to the wardroom to leave a bulky suitcase
he was carrying, and gave him a whisky and soda. Conversation was limited, as he knew little English. Then I led the
way up to the bridge and presented him to the Captain.

" No, no, this is the wrong General. I wish to see the Norwegian General. They tell me he is in the ship. I must report to him."

The Captain explained that no other Norwegian officer had been on board. The Colonel was evidently disappointed, and was about to leave when Number One appeared. He reported that the Commander-in-Chief of the Norwegian Army, General Ruge, and his staff were in the woods behind the town. He had asked them whether they wished to embark for England, but the General had refused to leave his country.

" Ah," said the Colonel, " that is my General ! I must go to him."

I had hardly seen him over the side when there was a cry of " Aircraft ! Take cover ! " which was repeated along the jetty and far into the town. I went to Y Gun and stood by, but nothing happened. Except for the crackling of the flames in a nearby church, all was still.

Then I heard the sound of an engine in the distance, and a moment later saw the headlights of a lorry moving down the mountain road behind the town. One of the sailors garrisoning M—— came up to the guardrail and said, " We're all so bloody windy here now, we jump at the slightest sound. They've bombed this place almost incessantly for the past five days. N.O.I.C. has moved his headquarters four times, and each time he's moved it the Germans have bombed the previous one within a few hours."

I went down to the wardroom for a sandwich and a whisky and soda, and saw that the Norwegian Colonel had left his suitcase behind him. Number One told me to find him and hand it back, so I went over the gangway, where the Petty Officer Telegraphist was having a heated discussion about wavelengths with a Norwegian who understood no English, and set off through the burning town.

I found the Colonel in a little clearing in the woods above M——. He was standing beside his Commander-in-Chief, and they were surrounded by the General's staff-officers,

10 NORWAY, MAY, 1940

11 OILING

12 CHIPPING THE PAINTWORK

There must have been nearly twenty officers in that group, but not one was speaking. They looked down vacantly at the burning town and the outline of *T——* alongside the jetty, and there was utter depression in their eyes. They stood like men in a dream, the suitcases which contained their entire possessions lying in the snow beside them. The glow of the fires lit up their grey-blue cloaks and peaked caps ; it was like a scene in a Ruritanian play. I put down the Colonel's suit-case beside him, but I do not think he noticed what I had brought him.

I took a last look at the little group as I walked down the hill to the ship ; the small figure of General Ruge seemed to dominate it. Later he went to Tromso, where he stayed until the end of the campaign, refusing offers of a passage to England. He was a brave and loyal man, but he paid for his loyalty. The Germans put him in a concentration camp.

By the time I got back to the ship the greater part of the garrison had been embarked in the *U——* ; an hour later we steamed out to sea. I watched the red glow in the sky above *M——* growing smaller until we reached the mouth of the fjord, when it vanished. Then, very tired, I went down to my cabin and threw myself on to my bunk. In a few seconds I was asleep.

Two days later we reached England.

CHAPTER TEN

PATROLS

I

We saw the Norwegian campaign through to the end. Our last base was at Harstad, near Narvik, from which we worked for nearly a month. We were screening the *Ark*, a job which brought no excitement and much hard work; but night watches were not so strenuous as usual, as daylight lasted for twenty-four hours at that time of year. Keeping a middle watch in bright sunshine was a queer sensation. . . .

Harstad looked a nice place, and those who had been ashore spoke highly of the girls, who were blonde, beautiful, and apparently knew all the answers. But we never stayed long enough to see for ourselves. It was a case of oiling, provisioning, and out again.

We went south at the end of that patrol for a long-awaited boiler clean. It was good to be home again, to see green grass and trees, and to sit lazily in the sun. It was good to lie in a comfortable bed until ten in the morning, eat fresh vegetables, drink fresh milk, take a girl dancing, play tennis and try to cram into five days all the things one had wanted to do for so long. But the time passed too quickly, and within ten days we were at sea, heading for Norway again. . . .

A few days later the Norwegian campaign ended, and we returned to harbour; we remained there for the rest of the summer except for a few short trips into the Atlantic and North Sea. After our long sea-time we found this pleasant at first. There were opportunities to visit our friends in the flotilla and depot-ships, and we got our mail regularly. We could get down to paper-work, which had been accumulating for the past two months—and we had eight hours' sleep, in pyjamas, every night.

But after a time the inactivity began to pall. There was

little to do ashore, as we were based on one of the most desolate harbours in the British Isles, and many of us felt that we would rather go to sea for five or six days than be continually slipping to proceed for exercises, oiling, shoving off and making fast again.

There were many things we missed, too : trees, green fields, shops, houses, people to talk to who weren't in the Navy and, above all, girls. There was so much time to think about them, and so little we could do about it. After two or three months we had almost forgotten how a woman walked, talked or looked. The trend of conversation in the wardroom deteriorated daily.

I used to get the bug out of my system by writing and, on the days we were in harbour, walking two or three miles across the hills to a loch, where I would spend the afternoon fishing. Even if the trout were not rising it was good to lie back on the heather by the waterside, watching the curlews and skuas wheel above me in the blue sky. Sometimes I would see the Admiral fishing from his boat at the far end of the loch, and once I think I actually saw him trolling.

Sometimes we went to sea for two or three days' anti-submarine patrol. It was fun if the weather was fine. I remember some happy middle watches on the bridge, when the sea was calm and the night bright with stars. Leaning on the front of the bridge, drinking the cups of cocoa the messenger brought up from time to time, I used to discuss many subjects with my fellow officer of the watch : sex, religion, the Navy, literature, art and the human emotions. One got to know one's messmates best that way. But there were other watches when the bows plunged furiously into a head sea, throwing sheets of spray over the bridge. The cocoa was late and lukewarm ; the Captain was in a bad temper ; one started the zig-zag the wrong way and threw everyone else out. Those watches were not so pleasant.

II

One day Henry and I had the first watch together. We had left harbour two days before for an A/S patrol in the Atlantic, taking B—— and M—— under our orders. As I came on watch, we had almost reached the position of patrol. It was a damp, misty evening and I envied the others in the wardroom.

Guns, whom I was relieving, had just explained to me the intricacies of the zig-zag. I wasn't sure if I had the hang of it and was working out the times and alterations on the back of a signal-pad when the Captain, who was on the other side of the bridge, suddenly asked, " Made a hash of the zig-zag ? " I thought for a moment he was referring to my figures, but looking up saw that B——, which was on our port beam, had turned the opposite way to us. However M——, which was to starboard, was steering our course.

I looked quickly at the zig-zag book. " No, sir," I said, " I think it's B—— who's made a hash of it this time."

" Oh, well," said the Captain, " keep a good eye on her. She'll probably come round in a minute or two."

Minutes passed, but B—— stuck to her course. The Captain turned to the yeoman. " Make to B—— ' Keep in proper station '," he ordered. The yeoman took up his Aldis and was about to pass the signal when B—— started calling us up. The yeoman answered with a succession of T's. " From B——, sir. ' Attention is called to bearing 030 degrees '."

We searched the horizon on either side of the bearing with our binoculars, but could see nothing.

" Make ' What can you see ? ' " ordered the Captain.

The reply came, " Object temporarily lost in mist, but am steering towards it."

" We'd better investigate this," said the Captain. " Hoist ' Turn together seventy degrees to port. Speed twenty-five knots '."

The yeoman translated the orders down the voicepipe to

the flagdeck, and the flags were run up on the halyards. *B—* and *M——* hoisted the main answer close up. "All answered, sir," reported the yeoman.

"Haul down," said the Captain. "Port twenty. Two four two revolutions."

B—— began flashing to us again as we made the turn. I read, "Object in sight now bearing 020 degrees. Am proceeding to investigate."

"I've got it," cried Spider, and we followed the line of his glasses. Seven or eight thousand yards away a speck was just visible on the surface of the water. We all began thinking the same thing : could it be a U-Boat charging her batteries on the surface? The Captain was taking no chances, for he ordered B Gun to load and the depth charges to be set.

The yeoman began flashing again. "From *B——*, sir. ' Object is ship's life-boat containing about a dozen people '."

"Right ! Set depth charges to safe. Speed fifteen knots."

Soon we could spot the lifeboat for ourselves. *B——*, now nearly a mile ahead of us, went cautiously alongside, and through my glasses I could see figures scrambling up the netting to her upper deck. The lifeboat was cast adrift. Then we reformed in line abreast and set course for our area of patrol.

A little later the yeoman wrote out a long signal from *B——*. "Survivors" it ran "are from Portuguese ship, torpedoed without warning five nights ago when sailing independently. Three survivors are suffering from gangrene and seriously ill. Master reports second boat last seen drifting north-west two days ago."

Although darkness was falling, the Captain decided to carry out a sweep to the northward in the hope of finding the second lifeboat ; ships were spread five miles apart and speed increased to twenty-seven knots. A man was placed in the crow's-nest, and the look-outs were instructed to sweep the horizon with their glasses.

We continued the search until night had fallen but saw

nothing, and at midnight turned to carry out our original objective, the A/S patrol.   Again we were unlucky, and the next afternoon set course for home.   Arrived in harbour a day later, B——'s Number One came over for a gin while we were alongside the oiler.   He told us that the survivors had just gone ashore in a drifter ; their gratitude had been almost embarrassing.   Most of them were still pretty ill ; they had run out of water two days before they were picked up.   One poor fellow had got gangrene badly, and the Doc thought that he would probably lose both legs and both hands. . . .

Our feelings were best expressed by the Captain.   At dinner that night he said, " The day we *do* run into a U-Boat, there won't be any question whether it's been sunk or not." But he didn't put it quite like that. . . .

III

At the beginning of September, 1940, we got the signal to proceed to D—— to refit.   For the past six weeks the ship had been alive with buzzes.   Some had said that we were going to refit in America ; others that we wouldn't refit until the New Year.   Everyone had his theory and firmly believed that it was the correct one.

Now there was no longer any doubt.   The Captain cleared lower deck and told the ship's company, between bursts of cheering, that there would probably be three weeks' leave to each watch ; that he would come down heavily on leave-breakers ; and that the ship would sail at noon.   At noon precisely we slipped from the buoy and, passing out of harbour, set course for the south.   I spent the next two days in the office with the writer and the coxswain making out ration cards, pay lists and railway warrants, and seeing that all was in readiness so that, directly the last shell was out of the ship, the first watch could proceed on leave.

We steamed down the Minches in glorious sunshine. Number One had put the sailors on to chipping the paint-work, and they whistled and sang as though they hadn't a care in the world. The atmosphere had changed in a day from lethargy to excitement and expectation. It affected the officers, too. Doc and I split a bottle of champagne at supper the first night out—an unwise move on my part as I had the morning watch, and overslept. Two days later we made fast alongside the jetty in D——.

LOFOTEN RAID

I

By Christmas we were back at sea, and with the New Year began a series of long, tiring trips into the Atlantic, escorting the battlewagons. The *Hipper* had been in action with the *Berwick* on Christmas Day, and the *Scharnhorst* and *Gneisenau* were reported on the move. The C.-in-C. was taking no chances.

We hated those trips. It was bloody cold, and the sea was usually rough. We were tossed from one side of the ship to the other, the food and the mess traps flew off the table, and by the end of a watch you were drenched to the skin.

God, how bored we were! If there had been some chance of action we wouldn't have minded the discomfort; but there wasn't. Watch—sleep—food was the invariable routine; but it kept us going. We had no time to think of the things we missed: homes, families, girls. And we lost all sense of time; the day might be Thursday, Sunday or Tuesday for all we knew or cared.

One day towards the end of February, 1941, when the ship was alongside the depot-ship, the Flotilla Gunnery Officer came into the wardroom and asked for Number One.

" He's out of the ship," I said. " Any message ? "

" Yes, tell him there's to be a G.C.O.'s conference at ten o'clock to-morrow."

A Gunnery Control Officers' conference ! What's that in aid of, I wondered ?

The mystery deepened next day when the Captain went over to see Captain (D) with the other captains of the flotilla, and later to a conference in the flagship with the C.-in-C. However, it was no good getting excited; that sort of thing

76

13   SVOLVAER, LOFOTEN ISLANDS, MARCH 4TH, 1941

14 THE LOFOTEN RAID : INVASION BARGES RETURNING FROM SHORE

had happened before and had usually resulted in nothing. I took the afternoon off and went ashore.

It was a fine, crisp day, and I enjoyed the long walk to the pub at L——, where I had tea and bought some fresh eggs. There was snow on the ground, and the air was sharp and invigorating.

When I returned to the ship, I went down to my cabin in the office flat. There I found Spider, knee-deep in confidential books.

" What in God's name are you up to ? " I asked.

" We're clearing the C.B.'s out of the ship," he answered. " It's all to do with this operation. Keep it under your hat as much as you can for the present. We'll all know about it to-morrow."

Next morning, after breakfast, I took the daily correspondence up to the Captain for signature. When I opened the door I saw that he and Spider were studying a big chart. He turned as I entered and said, " All right, I'll go through the bumph later on. I'm rather busy just now." I went down to the wardroom, where Henry told me that a brigadier and a marine officer were arriving on board that afternoon, and that the Captain wished to see all officers in his cabin at eleven o'clock. This looked like something exciting at last.

We began to speculate on what it could be. Someone suggested a landing in Denmark ; someone else a " death and glory " expedition into Trondheim. Spider came down with a bunch of papers in his hand. " Big stuff ! " he said. " The best thing we've done this war. But you'll hear all about it shortly."

At eleven o'clock we assembled in the Captain's cabin. The door was shut and locked, and we gathered round the table on which the chart was spread. It was labelled " Norway— North-West Coast."

" This is where we're going," said the Captain, and pointed to Svolvaer, the capital of the Lofoten Islands, ninety miles inside enemy territory. " The objects of the expedition are as follows. First, to sink as much German shipping as we

11

can find. Second, to capture the German garrisons. Third, to bring back to England as many Norwegian volunteers as want to come. Absolute secrecy has got to be maintained until we are at sea. If we get sighted by aircraft, then the whole party's off."

This was the kind of show we had been waiting for. At last we were taking the offensive, *we* were attacking the Germans instead of waiting for them to attack us. We felt like excited children. " This'll show the sods ! " we thought. " God, what a break ! "

II

The brigadier and the marine arrived that evening ; a little later we sailed. The voyage across the North Sea was uneventful ; the sea was calm all the way, the weather dull, and the clouds made visibility poor. That was just what we wanted.

The brigadier was very popular. We took him round the ship and showed him everything ; but what caught his imagination most were the Northern Lights, which he had never seen before. He spent a quarter of an hour on the quarterdeck one evening admiring them.

We were due to arrive off Svolvaer at dawn on the 4th March ; on the night of the third we began to make preparations for battle. After dinner I went down to my cabin to change into clean clothes. We usually do this when there is a chance of action, as wounds are more likely to fester if one has been wearing the same underclothes for two or three days. It always seems to me a cold-blooded business, like being shaved before an operation. I stripped to the skin, sponged myself over and put on silk vest and pants, long-legged woollen pants and a woollen vest over them, then a shirt, trousers, a couple of pullovers and my reefer. I filled my flask with brandy, stuffed a couple of bars of chocolate into the pocket of my duffel-coat and saw that I had plenty of matches and cigarettes. Then I emptied my pockets of letters and papers which might be of use to the enemy if I was captured.

The " brig " was in cracking form that evening. Before dark he had sent a signal to his opposite number in the troopship : " Hope to see you ashore to-morrow for a Schnapps." Now, over a final whisky and soda in the wardroom, he told me of his hopes for the success of the operation. " You've no idea," he said, " what a difference this party will make to *morale* inside the country if it's a success. The production of munitions will go up by leaps and bounds ; the workers will feel that the guns and shells they're making are really being used to good effect."

The others drifted into the wardroom to fill their flasks, and buy " Nutty " or a packet of cigarettes. Then the joking started.

" My address from to-morrow," said Henry, " will be Oflag VI B. Write me a line some time."

Someone else said, " Go and see my poor old mother and tell her my last thought was of her."

" My address," said Tiny, " will be care of D. Jones, Esq., The Locker, Vest Fjord."

" I wonder if there are any nice girls in Svolvaer ? "

" I'm going to get as whistled as a coot when we get back."

" Wonder if I'll be able to get ashore to-morrow all right," said the " brig."

We went to action stations. I climbed up on to the pompom deck and wedged myself on the gun-platform between the layer and trainer. We were inside the Arctic Circle now, and it was bitterly cold. I sent off the crew in twos and threes to get warm in the cabouche on X Gun Deck and took a swig of brandy for myself. It was a pitch-black night, thank God, and the forms of the destroyers on either side of us were hardly visible. After a while the cold became almost unbearable—a numbing cold which stupefied your brain and made you want to sleep. Several times I found my head lolling against the sighting bar.

I began talking to the captain of the gun to keep myself awake. He told me about gunboats in China, and the times he had had in Hong-Kong and Wei Hei Wei before the war.

He told me of his wife in Belfast and of his love for his native country, Ireland. He told me about the West Indies Station, and an American girl he had nearly married in Bermuda. Then he said, " Look at them lights, sir ! "

Off the port bow lights began to appear through the darkness ; I knew then that we were entering Vest Fjord, the long channel which is the approach to the iron-ore town of Narvik. Soon the lights were abreast of us, scores of them—green, red and white.

" Just like Piccadilly —— Circus," said one of the crew.

It must have been about five o'clock when the whine of the engines took on a deeper note and I knew that we were reducing speed. We stopped as dawn was breaking. I could just distinguish the outlines of mountains towering above us to port, and at the foot of one black smudges which were houses.

It was absolutely still ; not a sound anywhere now that our engines were stopped. I heard quite clearly an officer in the troopship giving orders for the lowering of the invasion craft. There was a creaking of ropes as the davits were swung out and the boats lowered into the water. They moved off noiselessly like ghosts towards the town.

Dawn broke, and brought one of the loveliest sights I have ever seen. To port, stretching in either direction as far as I could see, was range upon range of mountains, covered with snow. To starboard and astern were the flat, blue waters of Vest Fjord and, across the fjord, the snow-capped mountains of the mainland. The sun appeared from behind the mountains and shone from a blue, cloudless sky.

Suddenly I heard the whine of the gun pumps, and saw that the main armament was being brought to bear on the starboard bow. A small coasting vessel was making its way out of harbour ; through my glasses I saw the Nazi flag flying at the stern. She crossed our bows and, believing T—— to be a German warship, dipped her flag in salute. Had she observed us closely she would have seen the battle ensign fluttering at our foremast.

Our reply was to send a shot across her bows. She sheered off at that; a little later a boat was slung out and the crew abandoned ship. Number One opened up with the forward guns, and soon the ship was a blazing mass; she ran aground on some rocks and burnt herself out. We heard later that her captain had committed suicide.

The Norwegian fishing fleet of thirty or forty small trawlers chugged past us on its way out to the fishing grounds. As the trawlers passed the fishermen stood up, waving their caps in the air and cheering wildly. Several boats came alongside, and I saw our messman striking a bargain over some cod.

By now the Army had gained possession of the town. We had heard no shots, so presumed that the capture had been bloodless. It turned out later that most of the Germans were caught in bed.

The Army had posted a signalman on the roof of one of the tallest houses, and soon we were maintaining regular communication, although I couldn't make out what he was flashing, as the ship was under helm most of the time and we were keeping a sharp air look-out. The Captain next turned his attention to a large merchant ship which lay at anchor behind the rocks fringing the outer harbour. Another warning shot across the bows to give the crew time to abandon ship; then, steaming slowly up and down the outer roads, we shelled her until she sank in flames at her moorings. It was grand to see the streaks of flame shooting mast-high as the shells burst on her sides, and to watch her list farther to starboard, until she lurched suddenly beneath the surface. We heard later that this ship was a floating fish-oil factory, and was manufacturing large quantities of refined oil for use in explosives.

Alongside her was another smaller ship which, as luck would have it, had been loading cases of fish and was due to sail for Germany that day. She, too, was sent to the bottom in a very short time. Smaller vessels which were out of sight behind the rocks were dealt with by the Commandos.

The morning wore on. Occasionally I heard sounds of firing up and down the fjord from other ships in the flotilla;

we wondered if they were having as good a time as we were. Suddenly there was a tremendous explosion from the shore, and the big fish-oil refinery was enveloped in a cloud of thick, black smoke. It cleared gradually and formed into a wide spiral which rose high into the air, contrasting with the white background of the mountains. The demolition party had done its job.

Nine o'clock—ten o'clock—eleven o'clock; some of the invasion barges from inshore began heading towards us. Through my glasses I could see figures standing in them—not soldiers, but a queer assortment of civilians, and nondescripts wearing all kinds of uniform. As they approached, an officer in one of them hailed the ship. " Germans and quislings ! Can you accommodate them temporarily ? "

The boat came alongside and the prisoners began swarming over the side. Tiny, whose action station was at X Gun, and I went down to the upper deck to supervise. I pointed my revolver into the middle of the crowd and assumed an expression of determination and, I hope, ruthlessness. This was to cover the fact that I had forgotten to put any ammunition into the chamber.

Another A.L.C. came along the starboard side and emptied itself of a crowd of Norwegian volunteers. We put the volunteers on one side of the torpedo tubes, the Germans and quislings on the other; I marched up and down with my revolver. The Germans were a mixed crowd—two or three airmen from the seaplane base, a few soldiers, one in the uniform of the Alpine Corps, and a good many merchant seamen, mostly from the ships we had sunk, wearing " Kriegsmarine " on their cap-ribbons. The quislings were in civilian clothes—cheap cloth suits and trilby hats. One was in the uniform of the Norwegian police and wore a black Cossack cap. The officer in the A.L.C. said, " Keep a good eye on him, he's the worst of the lot."

" Pretty dismal lot of ——s, aren't they, sir ? " one of the sentries remarked. And that just about summed them up.

III

How the " brig " got ashore I don't know, because the Captain had refused to lower any of the ship's boats, and I hadn't seen any A.L.C.'s come alongside on their way to the town.   But he was determined to go ashore, and by some means best known to himself, he did.   Now he was climbing on board again.   I helped him over the guardrail.

" How are things going ashore ? " I asked him.

" Splendidly ; couldn't be better !   We took them completely by surprise.   As far as I know, our only casualty is a man who shot himself in the foot by mistake."

" And what about the Schnapps ? "

" Well, we went to the local, and the old woman who ran it told us she knew that we were coming some day and had saved up a bottle for the occasion.   Only it wasn't Schnapps ; it was Sandeman's port, which she thought we'd like better. We split the bottle, and made everybody else in the pub drink our health.   Then they had their breakfast."

The " brig " also told me that the officer detailed to cut the telephone wires couldn't resist sending a telegram before doing so.   It ran, " To A. Hitler, Berchtesgarten.   Here we are in Svolvaer.   What are you going to do about it ? *Signed* ——, Lieutenant."   The " brig " then went forward to see the Captain.   He was at the top of his form.

A small Norwegian fishing-boat came alongside, and a man who appeared to be in a state of great agitation came aboard. He told us that both his sons were among those volunteering to return to England ; they were only little boys of twelve and thirteen and their mother was frantic.   I found them for him —hulking youths who looked as though they could have felled and eaten an ox.   He hustled them into the boat and made off.

Twelve o'clock—half-past ; the time-limit for our stay was nearing.   The A.L.C.'s came to collect the prisoners and volunteers, to re-embark them in the troopships.   Captain (D) hoisted his course and speed, and we began the long journey down Vest Fjord. All that could be seen of Svolvaer as we steamed away was a pall of thick, black smoke rising into the clear air, high above the mountains. As we passed down the coastline of the Lofotens, other smudges told of the destruction of German-controlled industries and plants.

Towards evening, when we had been at action stations for nearly twenty hours, a single German aircraft appeared, circled round us several times and flew away. It was the only time we sighted the enemy during the course of the operation.

Darkness fell and the watch was piped to defence stations. The journey back to harbour was uneventful. The day we arrived in harbour we received a signal from the C.-in-C.; the yeoman answered him with the twenty-inch.

" Pass to all concerned. I congratulate you. . . ."

15 SCREENING *ARK ROYAL*

16 TRIBAL DESTROYER

17, 18   MAY 27TH, 1941 :   THE LAST HOURS OF *BISMARCK*; *T——'S* BATTLE ENSIGN AT THE
FOREMAST

CHAPTER TWELVE

BATTLE IN THE ATLANTIC

One evening, towards the end of May, 1941, we were escorting the battleship *Rodney* across the Atlantic; I was on watch, and nothing of interest was happening. I was checking up on my bearing and distance for perhaps the sixth time when I heard the buzzer from the wireless office indicating that a signal was ready. The signalman of the watch, a barrel-shaped fellow and an inveterate gambler off whom I had won many bars of " Nutty," thrust his huge fist into the voicepipe and hauled up the signal box. He unravelled the signal, scanned it, then,

" Blimey, sir," he said, " look at this ! "

There was not much on that signal, only a few coded letters and figures ; but a glance told me that the German battleship *Bismarck* had been sighted by our cruisers patrolling the Denmark Strait. From then the signals poured in. We discussed the situation in the wardroom that night after dinner, and continued talking into the early hours of the morning.

It usually takes my servant several minutes to rouse me, but when he called me at eight o'clock I was wide awake.

" 'Eard the news, sir ? " he said. " The *'Ood's* gone."

That was a hard blow, as we had screened *Hood* many times ; but it failed to damp our spirits. It filled us with a greater determination to make contact with *Bismarck* and engage her.

After breakfast the Gunner and I went up to the chart-house. Spider had placed a large-scale chart of the Atlantic on the board ; we could see *Bismarck's* course through the Denmark Strait plotted from the positions given by the shadowing cruisers ; we could see where *Hood* had been sunk and, moving southwards, our own position. Spider had also marked the positions and courses of our heavy ships as they raced from all parts of the Atlantic to head off the enemy.

As the day passed, we realised that, if we were to alter course to the northward and *Bismarck* were to continue on her present course, we would probably be the first to engage her. Sure enough, when I came up for the afternoon watch we had altered course and were rapidly closing the enemy.

We steamed north-westwards all that day, the seas getting higher, the wind rising, hourly. When I came on watch again at midnight it was blowing a full gale. *Rodney* had left us behind, and was out of sight ahead in the blackness.

Then came the news that *Bismarck* had shaken off her pursuers in the dark. This was depressing, as we had expected to go into action within the next twenty-four hours. The question now arose which port *Bismarck* was making for; would she double back on her tracks and return to Norway, passing between Iceland and the Faroes, or would she continue southwards towards Brest? Every Flag and Commanding Officer of the British forces afloat sensed that she would press on southwards. It was a gamble, of course, but in turning southwards the Commander-in-Chief took a chance which was later justified.

I came off watch at four o'clock to find my cabin in chaos. Even my little wireless, which was firmly wedged in the bookcase, had fallen off its shelf and joined the rest of my possessions on the deck. I think that watch was the most unpleasant I have ever kept.

We steamed southwards all the next day, wondering where *Bismarck* had got to and very much afraid that she had eluded us. The sighting report of the patrolling Catalina did nothing to raise our spirits, for it showed that *Bismarck* was many miles south of us, steaming at a comfortable speed towards Brest.

Then something happened which, in a moment, altered the situation. Late on the evening of the 26th, a torpedo-carrying aircraft from *Ark Royal*, which had left Gibraltar at short notice, scored a direct hit on *Bismarck's* stern, smashing her propellers, jamming her rudder and flooding her steering compartment. The ship turned helplessly in two wide circles; then, her speed greatly reduced, steadied on her original course.

We now knew for certain that it was only a matter of time before we made contact. I think we all felt a bit apprehensive as we closed up at action stations. It was a dark, gusty night, blowing hard; those in exposed positions were drenched by sheets of spray. Before dark, the Commander-in-Chief in *K.G. Five* had thundered over the horizon to join us, and now, from my action station at the pom-pom, I could just make out the vast, reassuring shapes of the two battlewagons astern.

I began wondering, as I had often done before, what this action would be like from my point of view. If we came upon *Bismarck* during the night the destroyers would go in to deliver a torpedo attack. I can't say that I looked forward to that, standing in one of the most exposed positions in the ship, with nothing else to occupy my mind. However, I thought of the *Rawalpindi*, and determined to be brave. It was a comfort to know that everyone else was probably just as frightened.

As events turned out it fell to the Fourth Flotilla, under the command of Captain Vian, to deliver the night attack. I heard this over the pom-pom telephone at about four in the morning, and we cheered when we learnt that the attack had been successful.

We remained at action stations all that night. At about nine the next morning I was on my way down to the ward-room for breakfast when I heard someone shout, " There she goes ! " Turning, I saw a puff of brown smoke suspended above *Rodney's* main armament; a moment later I heard the boom of her guns. The battle was on.

I wish I could describe adequately the scene that morning when the battleships came upon their quarry. I think it was the colour contrasts which impressed me most. It was one of those chilly, blustering days, when the sun shines intermittently from a blue sky between racing, white clouds. The sea was the colour of an emerald, the waves flecked with white foam. In the centre of the picture was *Bismarck*, black and massive, smoke and flames rising in spurts from between her decks. Around her, like wolves around their prey, lay the British warships, their grey sides glinting in the morning sun. From time to time we saw brilliant orange flashes from the heavy guns of *Rodney* and *K.G. Five*; they were followed by white fountains of spray, rising like mushrooms above the water; and a little later we saw brown puffs of cordite smoke dissolving in the sky.

We took no active part in the battle, but as spectators we had a ring-side seat. *Bismarck* fired spasmodically at the beginning of the action, then ceased firing altogether. She withstood terrible punishment from *Rodney* and *K.G. Five*; the scenes below her decks must have been frightful.

Of all forms of warfare, a sea-battle is the most impersonal. In hurling shells at an enemy who may be up to fifteen miles away you cannot feel much personal animosity towards him. I found it difficult to realise that inside that huge hulk across the water were nearly two thousand enemy sailors.

I think that all of us were willing to acknowledge the gallantry of the enemy. For the past five days the crew of *Bismarck* had been almost continually at action stations. She had been shadowed by our cruisers for nearly two days, shadowed and attacked by aircraft and, the night before the battle, subjected to a torpedo attack by the Fourth Flotilla. All through that night her crew must have known that dawn would bring the British Battle Fleet and, for most of them, death. I do not think you will find one British sailor present at the battle who will not admit that *Bismarck* fought a very gallant fight.

We left just before the end of the action. I took a last look at *Bismarck* as we steamed away. Through my glasses I could see great, jagged holes in her sides and superstructure, through which tongues of flame were shooting; she was listing heavily to port, emitting a column of black smoke.

Her guns were awry, some of them pointing meaninglessly to the sky. It was a terrible sight. *Bismarck* had been a majestic and powerful ship; now she was a charred and battered wreck.

All of us were relieved that the tension of the last four days was lifted, and showed our relief by pointless, good-humoured banter in the wardroom. For me, perhaps the battle had a more personal meaning than for the others; I felt I had been something more than a privileged spectator at a great sea fight. My mind went back to a cold, dark evening in November, 1939, when an armed merchant-cruiser, patrolling the blockade lines as *Norfolk* and *Suffolk* had done, had gone down in flames at the hands of another German battleship, her guns firing and her colours flying to the last.

And I felt, somehow, that I had seen *Rawalpindi* avenged. . . .

CHAPTER THIRTEEN

BATTLE IN THE AIR

" Half-past seven, sir ! Wake up, Mr. Kennedy, sir, it's half-past seven and you've got the forenoon watch ! " I turn over in my bunk sleepily. " All right, messenger, I'm awake. Is the navigating officer keeping relieve decks ? "

" Yes, sir. You will be required on the bridge at half-past eight."

I lie in my bunk for a few minutes, my mind full of the events of the last four days. What a chase *Bismarck* led us, and what a sight the battle was ! We shall be in harbour by this evening and, if I know the Captain, there will be some party.

I hoist myself out of my bunk and go to the washstand to get the sleep out of my eyes and brush my teeth. I pull on my trousers, get into my reefer and brush my hair. Then I hurry to the wardroom for breakfast.

Broad, the duty steward, is sitting in one of the armchairs reading *Life*. " Come on, Broad," I say, " I want my breakfast. Is it ready ? "

" Just coming down, sir," says Broad ; that is his stock answer to enquiries about food. What he really means is, " It will be placed in front of you as soon as I go up to the galley and collect it from that fat cook."

I drink a cup of tea while Broad is up at the galley and switch on the wireless. A man is encouraging me to grip the bars of a chair and kick my legs sideways in time with the music he is going to play. In a few minutes Broad comes down with breakfast.

I am well into my second egg when Guns, who has been having the morning watch, comes in for a cup of tea before changing. " What's it like up there this morning ? " I ask him.

" Grand ! " says Guns. " Sun's shining, not too cold,

quite dry on the bridge. Captain's in a good temper and all's well with the world. We ought to be in by tea-time."

" What price the Locarno this evening ? " I ask him.

" No, just a few pints in a quiet little pub will do me nicely, I think," says Guns.

" And with a nice quiet little something to hold your hand, I daresay."

" I'm a respectable married man, I am," says Guns, winking.

" Yes, indeed ! "   He winks again.

I finish my breakfast and go back to my cabin for my duffel-coat, gloves and binoculars. I come out on to the quarterdeck and make my way forward.

It is a crisp, bright morning, much the same as yesterday though there are more clouds in the sky, and the wind is stronger. It biffs me hard from the other side of the funnel-casing and machine-gun bridge as I walk along the upper deck.

" 'Morning Spider," I say, as I climb on to the compass platform beside him. " What's happening ? "

" Nothing much," Spider answers. " Course 026, speed 15 knots, 142 revolutions. H.A. cruising stations. M—— a mile on the starboard beam."

M—— is our chummy ship, and no doubt we will celebrate with her when we get in this evening.

I am just going to take over the watch officially from Spider when I see him looking intently through his glasses towards the starboard quarter. " I don't like the look of that," he says. " Can you see what it is ? "

I raise my glasses and train them in the same direction. Almost immediately, a big, black, four-engined aeroplane appears in the field of vision. I can see the black crosses on the fuselage distinctly.

" Christ, yes," I say. " It's a mucking Wulf ! "

" I'll tell the Master," Spider says. " You ring the alarm bells."

I go to the front of the bridge and press the alarm push : *short long, short long, short long*—the signal for anti-aircraft action stations.

When the Captain reaches the bridge I run down to my action station at the pom-pom. My crew are manning the telephones, seeing that the feed belts are in order, setting the levers to fire. I climb to the middle of the platform between the trainer and captain of the gun and the layer.

The Focke-Wulf cruises round, but remains at some distance, out of range of the main armament. I post look-outs on either quarter in case dive-bombers come shooting out of the low clouds. Keeping a watchful eye all round I await further developments.

I do not have to wait long ; the port look-out reports an aircraft approaching from the port beam. I look up, and recognise it as a Heinkel III. A moment later, Number One in the Director lets fly with the main armament. That scares the pilot, for he turns away without finishing his run.

" Aircraft to starboard, sir," shouts one of the loading numbers.

" Train right," I order.

The trainer moves his handle as fast as he can, and in a few seconds the gun is brought round to face the starboard bow. Two Heinkel III's are approaching, about three thousand feet up on a level course. The main armament is training round to engage, but they will not be able to get off a salvo in time. It is up to us.

I wait until the planes are within effective gun range, then give the order, " Open fire ! " The staccato bark of the guns usually deafens me ; now I can hardly hear it. I am too intent on watching those black vultures coming to the end of their run.

Now I can see the bombs falling. They are specks at first, like sparrows' eggs, but grow larger every second. The Captain has seen them, too, for we are moving faster and heeling over to port as we swing to starboard. I clutch the stanchion and watch the bombs, fascinated.

" It's all right, chaps," I yell, " they won't hit us ! "

Woomph, woomph, woomph ; the bombs have landed in our wake and have burst with tremendous detonations. The

Captain brings the ship back to her original course, and by the low-pitched whine from the gearing-room I can tell that we are reducing speed.

We have hardly finished engaging this pair when two more appear on the port bow. And so it goes on ; the guns fire, the aircraft drop their bombs, the ship swings to port or starboard, and the bombs land in the sea, sometimes quite far away, at other times too close to be comfortable.

During a lull Petty Officer J—— turns and says : " Looks as though they've hit M——, sir ! " Poor old M——! She has taken a list to port, and clouds of steam are rising from abreast the break of the fo'c'sle. The list increases, and she has soon stopped altogether. Thank God those filthy aeroplanes are giving us a respite now, just when we need it !

We close to within two cables of M——, which has now listed over forty degrees, and I intercept a signal from her, " Abandoning ship." A little later, figures can be seen sliding down her hull into the water.

I go down to the upper deck to help Number One super-intend the placing of nets over the ship's side. The cooks have left their supply parties and are preparing hot soup in the galleys. The doctor is turning the wardroom into a second sick-bay. Blankets are being stripped from the officers' bunks and piled in a corner.

The first survivors reach the ship. We haul them up the netting and deposit them on the upper deck, where their wet clothes are stripped from their shivering bodies. They are wrapped in blankets and taken to the wardroom or the Captain's day-cabin to be rubbed down. Some of the older men have not the strength to cover the whole journey ; when they have almost reached the netting they seem to think that they are saved and do not bother to exert themselves more. This is fatal, because they begin to sink at once and then they must make an even greater effort to right themselves.

For a whole hour we lie stopped, while exhausted men, in twos and threes, reach the ship's side and are helped on board. Last off his ship is M——'s Captain ; he is pushing two exhausted men on a rubber cushion in front of him, and from time to time stops to wave his ship's battle-ensign and shout encouragement to the others.

We are all wondering what has happened to the German bombers. Surely they must return soon ; and God help us when they do !

M—— is lying on her side now, motionless and broken, like a wounded animal awaiting the end. We steam slowly away, leaving another destroyer, which has joined us, to send her to the bottom by gunfire. We set course for harbour.

I go down to the wardroom to give the doctor a hand, but have not been there more than a few minutes when I hear the cry : " Aircraft approaching from astern ! " I am up at the pom-pom in a flash, and see another H.E. III flying dead up the stern. As soon as it reaches its position of bomb-release the Captain begins to swing the ship. The bombs start falling—*one*, *two*, *three*, *four*, *five*, I count. They seem to be coming straight at us. Christ ! They *are* going to hit us !

I hear myself shouting automatically, as I have done before : " It's all right ! They've missed again ! " Then the bombs land ; they fall in a little clump not fifty feet off the port quarter. They make no noise and there are no explosions— just five little *phuts* as they disappear beneath the surface. Thank God for the Czechs !

We are attacked all that afternoon, not incessantly but at about ten-minute intervals. I don't feel frightened while we are being attacked ; I am too fascinated by what is happening, too busy giving orders to my crew. Fear comes during the lulls ; it is when I hear the cry " Aircraft approaching " that I feel weak inside. It is the same feeling I had at school, waiting outside the headmaster's study to be beaten—a sickly, sinking sensation in the stomach. Only it is not as bad as that, because at school I wasn't allowed to alter course and increase speed to avoid what was coming to me ; I knew I had to take it.

Everyone is asking where our fighters are. We have been in sight of the Irish coast for two or three hours, and there is

19 MAY 28TH, 1941 : *M——'S* CAPTAIN SHORTLY AFTER HIS
RESCUE WITH THE CAPTAIN OF *T——*

20 POM-POM CREW AT ACTION STATIONS

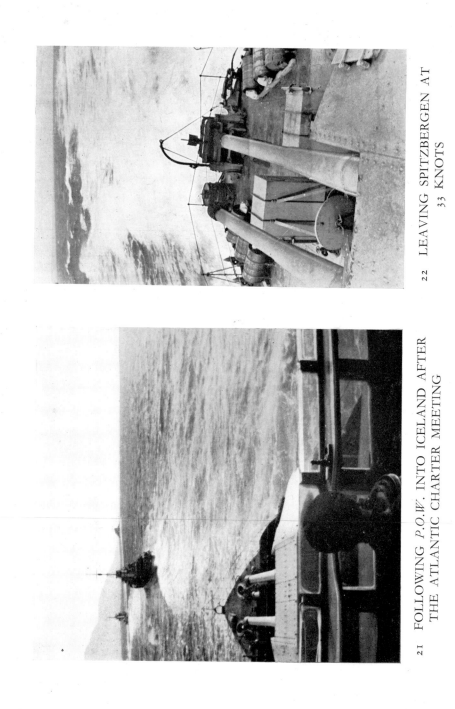

21 FOLLOWING *P.O.W.* INTO ICELAND AFTER
THE ATLANTIC CHARTER MEETING

22 LEAVING SPITZBERGEN AT
33 KNOTS

still no sign of them. During a lull at about five o'clock, a petty officer comes round with hot tea and ship's biscuits, the first food of the day for most of us. We crunch the dry biscuits hungrily and swallow gulps of the hot, sweet tea. After a cigarette we feel like new men.

Soon after, while a new attack is developing, we see a Hudson streaking across the sky—the first friendly aircraft that has been near us. It goes straight for an H.E. III which is about to attack the other destroyer, now four miles astern of us. Streams of smoke pour out of the Heinkel's fuselage, and we watch it plunge into the sea. A roar goes up from every man in the ship.

Just before nightfall another Hudson arrives to escort us into harbour. It circles around until dark, chasing off two more Heinkels which are manœuvring to attack. There is something unbelievably comforting in that fat, friendly, protecting form. I feel I would like to fall on the pilot's neck and weep with gratitude.

We enter harbour at midnight and make fast alongside the oiler. I walk stiffly down to the wardroom, which looks like the remains of a jumble-sale. " A whisky and soda, Broad," I say, " and make it a double."

" Aye, aye, sir," says Broad. " No party to-night, I'm afraid, sir."

" No, Broad, not to-night, but we'll make it an extra big one to-morrow."

We do. But that is another story. . . .

CHAPTER FOURTEEN

SPITZBERGEN

I

We had received a signal that morning from the Flag Officer Commanding Force—" Raise steam for twenty-four knots and be ready to follow me out of harbour at 1800." Shortly before we were due to sail the Captain had gone over to see R.A. (D) for last-minute orders.

We had speculated in the usual way on where we were going: Iceland? Russia? Someone had even suggested Nova Zembla. Our only clue had come from the Captain earlier in the day; " It'll probably be pretty cold," he had said. But that might be almost anywhere.

The motor-boat was bringing the Captain back to the ship. As officer of the day I saluted him as he came aboard. " Everything ready for sea ? " he asked.

" Yes, sir. Chief and Number One are ready, and we're on the slip rope."

The Captain went forward along the starboard side of the upper deck. Chief appeared from his bridge above the engine-room hatch. " Main engines ready, sir," he said.

" Righto, Chief. We're off now."

I followed the Captain up to the bridge. " All ready, Spider ? " he asked.

" Yes, sir."

" Ring on main engines."

The petty officer of the fo'c'sle raised his hammer and, on the order " Slip " from the Captain, knocked out the pin holding the slip-rope to the buoy. " Half ahead port—half astern starboard—one-one-o revolutions—starboard twenty." The bows pointed towards the harbour entrance.

" Stop starboard—midships—half ahead together." We were passing the depot-ship now. The yeoman said, " R.A.

(D) on the quarterdeck, sir." The piping-party piped the " still," and the Captain turned to salute. The Admiral and his chief of staff stood to attention on the quarterdeck of the depot-ship and saluted back. Then they piped the " Carry on."

The ship cleared the boom. " Out of harbour," shouted the yeoman down the voicepipe to the wireless office. " Pack up on port wave " ; and to the flag-deck, " Pendants down."

We joined the rest of the force outside the harbour and took up appointed station on the flagship. " Well boys," said the Captain, " the password this trip is Blitz Spitz."

Most of us had heard of Spitzbergen but no one knew exactly where it was. We got out the old wardroom atlas, a tattered volume which had been used on many similar occasions. " Seventy-eight north," someone said. " Won't be any too warm."

" Wonder if there's any chance of buying a huskie ? " said the Chief. " I would love a huskie."

" Or a baby polar bear," said someone else.

We steamed northwards that day and all the next ; then we began to enter the fog-banks. Ships took station in line ahead, and the quartermaster had orders to follow the next in the line. Sometimes the fog was so thick that visibility was reduced to less than a cable ; then a look-out was placed in the bows, and we followed the wake or, if we could see it, the fog-lamp, watching, watching all the time, ready to come down two or three turns instantly.

When the fog lifted we resumed our previous stations. About noon on the fourth day the Doc, who had been on deck for a breather, bounded into the wardroom and said, " Well, we're there ! "

We went up on deck to see for ourselves. Away on the starboard bow snowcapped mountains reared their summits above the horizon. The sea was a flat calm, the air crisp and clear as it always is in those parts. The mountains showed up distinctly.

I went up to the bridge. Spider said, " We're being sent

in first to see what's there. The rest of the force will be about twenty miles astern of us."

"Anybody got an idea what *is* there?" I asked.

"No, that's the thing. It may be full of Germans, or it may not. The Narvik flotilla may be there, or again it may not. It's our job to find out."

We went to action stations an hour later, and steamed towards the mouth of Isfjord, the big channel which gives access to the interior of the southern part of Spitzbergen. Now I could see the mountains more clearly; they presented a picture of utter desolation. The summits were covered with snow, but the bare sides were scaled with black, shapeless rock. Glaciers had formed between the peaks.

We stopped at the entrance to Isfjord, where a small wireless station had been established on a rocky promontory. The whaler was lowered, and an armed landing-party sent ashore to find out the lie of the land. The leading signalman went with it, taking a portable box lamp, and was soon flashing to the ship. I read: "No Germans in Spitzbergen," and told the crew; we were all relieved at the news. The feeling that the five destroyers of the Narvik flotilla might be waiting round the corner had not been pleasant.

While we were hoisting the whaler, the rest of the squadron appeared over the horizon and we entered Isfjord together. Some little way down it a channel branches off to the right. This leads to Barentsburg, the Russian settlement. Here half the squadron left us.

We continued down the fjord to Longyearby, the Norwegian settlement. On either side of us rose barren mountains; there were no trees, no vegetation, no signs of human or animal life; just mountains, rocks and glaciers. "'Ope we don't stay 'ere long, sir," said one of the crew.

We rounded a bend and, some way ahead of us at the end of the fjord, saw Longyearby. A medium-sized steamer was anchored off the jetty and, to the right, a long line of coal-pulleys stretched along the coast and into the mountains.

We made fast alongside the jetty in shallow water, and the

23   SPITZBERGEN : THE ARMED LANDING PARTY LEAVING TO SEIZE THE WIRELESS STATION

24 THE PRIME MINISTER COMING ABOARD *T*——
FROM *P.O.W.*

25 ESCORTING THE PRIME MINISTER IN *P.O.W*
THROUGH THE ATLANTIC CONVOY

inhabitants flocked out of their timber houses to greet us. Somehow we had expected them to appear in woad and skins ; but they wore much the same clothes as Norwegians I had seen elsewhere. They looked fit and well.

Olsen, our Norwegian cook, jumped down on to the jetty, and a crowd gathered round him as he told them our purpose in coming. Doc went ashore to visit the hospital and report on it. He was away some time, and when he returned we accused him, rather unkindly, of having flirted with the nurses.

The afternoon wore on. Among the crowd were several pretty girls, and one of them, whose lips and fingernails were, surprisingly, daubed with cosmetics, waved a coloured hand-kerchief she wore on her head. Some of the sailors, goofing on the upper deck, made signs to show that they wished to possess it. Cigarettes and chocolate were flung over the side in handfuls ; these the girl artfully picked up without parting with her handkerchief. Number One appeared and read the Riot Act, and peace was restored.

Having made a thorough investigation of the settlement and obtained the necessary information, we set sail again down the fjord. At the entrance leading to Barentsburg we were joined by the rest of the squadron. They had received an enthusiastic welcome from the Russians. One of the ships had approached the town flying the White Ensign and Hammer and Sickle at the fore, and had later turned out the marine band to play Russian national airs. P——, one of our sister ships, having no band, had dug out an old record of " O Tchechornya," which was played over and over again on the S.R.E., to the delight of the Russians.

We formed up on the flagship outside the mouth of the fjord, and soon the desolate coast of Spitzbergen had vanished over the horizon. Three weeks later a second expedition visited the island and blew up everything that might be of value to the enemy. But they were not troubled by the thought that five Narvik class destroyers might be waiting for them in Isfjord. . . .

II

The King visited the Fleet in August, 1941, and we had the honour of escorting the destroyer in which he was travelling to the embarkation port. Then, in company with two other destroyers, we set course for the west.

At first we thought that this was another dreary trip into the Atlantic to escort one of the battlewagons home ; in a sense it was. We had orders to proceed to a certain position in the North Atlantic to escort the battleship *Prince of Wales* to Iceland. It wasn't until later that we learnt that the Prime Minister and the British General Staff were on board her, returning from the Atlantic Charter meeting with President Roosevelt.

I had the morning watch when we made contact. It was a beautiful, clear day, with hardly a cloud in the sky and visibility about fifteen miles. A wisp of smoke above the horizon was the first indication that we had sighted the squadron ; then the masts of two escorting destroyers appeared and, a little later, the fighting top of *Prince of Wales*.

Half an hour later the destroyers reformed in a new screening diagram and, as senior officer of the escort, we took station ahead of *P.O.W.* Two American destroyers took station on either bow.

During the forenoon *P.O.W.* put up an impressive display of H.A. fire, shooting with great accuracy at target smoke-shell bursts. Later in the day the squadron altered course to starboard to close one of our large, homeward-bound, Atlantic convoys. We came upon it that evening, when the sun was sinking below the western horizon—line upon line of ships strung out in a long, well-formed line. It was the biggest convoy I had seen ; it consisted of ships of every nationality, loaded down to the waterline with tanks, aeroplanes, munitions and supplies. We turned and steamed through the lines at 25 knots into the setting sun. It was an impressive sight. *P.O.W.* ran up the signal "Pleasant voyage from Churchill!" and the Commodore of the convoy hoisted

V for Victory. When we had passed through once, the squadron was turned 180 degrees to starboard and we steamed back through the lines. Then we set course for Iceland, entering harbour in line ahead the following morning.

The Prime Minister was taken in another destroyer to Reykjavik, where he spent the day with the garrison of the island. That evening, in a rough sea and with a rising glass, we sailed for home.

On arrival in harbour two days later, the Captain took the ship skilfully alongside *P.O.W.*; we were to have the honour of taking the party the last stage of the journey to the port where it would catch the London train. The Prime Minister addressed the ship's company of *P.O.W.* from the quarterdeck; then, bidding goodbye to the C.-in-C., stepped on board and was taken up to the bridge. He was joined there by Sir John Dill, Sir Wilfrid Freeman and Sir Dudley Pound; there was only just room for the Captain and Spider to con the ship. I went up to the Director and took a photograph, but I was scared that someone might look round and spot me. In consequence, it didn't come out very well.

We cast off from *P.O.W.* and proceeded out of harbour at twenty-five knots. The Prime Minister stayed on the bridge until we had cleared the boom; then he went down to the Captain's cabin to rest, and buried himself in a three-day-old copy of *The Times*. Later, he spoke to me about the *Rawalpindi*. "That was a terrible thing," he said. " The A.M.C.'s have suffered more than any other class of ship."

We dropped anchor outside the harbour at noon, and a boat came alongside to take the party ashore. Then we returned to the base. I went fishing in the loch that evening and caught a two-pound trout.

CHAPTER FIFTEEN

NEW YEAR

It is 6.30 p.m. on the 31st December, 1941. In an hour's time I shall stop writing, call for my servant and, with his help, dress up as an Hawaiian native. The Petty Officer of my division has made me a hula skirt out of a length of ship's rope, and Cookie has given me cocoa from the galley to smear over my body. The Ordnance Artificer has promised me a necklace made of an old bicycle chain on which he has hung nuts, bolts, rings and other odds and ends from his workshop.

There is to be a fancy-dress party to celebrate the New Year. We shall all drink more than is good for us and to-morrow our heads will hum like cement-mixers. I only hope that we are not ordered suddenly to sea.

Meanwhile, it seems an appropriate time to think over the events of the last two years. For all that can be said against it, I am convinced that this war has done me good. It has taught me—and I imagine most of my contemporaries—many things, and brought me face to face with new aspects of life. Danger, for instance, and the imminence of death. I don't say that I am now so accustomed to the alarm bells sounding off action stations that they leave me unmoved, because fear is natural in the presence of danger. But I have occasionally been in great danger, and often in potential danger; and I am convinced that if, at any future time, I have to look death in the face, I shall be better prepared for it.

I have also had a certain amount of hardship. Life at Eton was jammy, at Oxford jammier still. In a destroyer in wartime it is far from jammy. You stand in stations exposed to the weather for long periods of the day and night; your rest and meals are frequently interrupted; the food is mostly tinned; you seldom see fresh milk or vegetables; and leave is scarce. Again, if in the future I find myself in a similar situation, I shall be better equipped to face it.

But the greatest gift the war has brought me is a sense of comradeship, which I did not know existed between men. In a ship you are bound closely to your messmates because you share a common danger with them. You work with them, eat with them, play with them; your lives are interwoven; on the fate of the ship depends the fate of each of you. It is a difficult feeling to describe, but perhaps it is best explained as a sense of mutual trust. *You* know you can depend on the other fellow; *he* knows he can depend on you. Neither will let the other down.

I have seen tragedy in this war, and I have seen beauty: dawn breaking over the grey Atlantic waters; middle watches on the bridge, the foremast swaying gently against a background of stars; the battlefleet manœuvring; destroyers steaming into a head sea; Northern Lights over an Icelandic fjord; the Lofoten Islands at daybreak. Those are sights which I shall never forget.

* * * * *

It is nearly midnight. My brother officers and I are standing in a ring on the quarterdeck. Opposite me the Captain is wearing silk pyjamas tucked into a pair of carpet slippers, an open shirt and a fez. Next to him the Chief is dressed as a Cossack and, next to the Chief, is the bulky figure of the Gunner (T), dressed as a clergyman.

They are my comrades of the war, with whom I live and work; they are my friends of the moment. I won't see most of my old friends until after the war.

The youngest member of the wardroom, Sub-Lieutenant J——, grips the clapper of the bell; a silence falls as midnight approaches. When the quartermaster of the watch says "Midnight, sir!" J—— strikes the bell firmly and evenly until the full sixteen strokes have been sounded. We join hands and sing "Auld Lang Syne."

I stay on the quarterdeck for a moment after the others have gone down to the wardroom. It is a still, peaceful night; a bright moon lights up the surface of the smooth, ice-cold water. Across the harbour I can see the shapes of other destroyers lying restlessly at their buoys. Their gun shields are silhouetted in the moonlight, the barrels trained on the fore-and-aft line of each ship.

"Auld Lang Syne" drifts across the water from another destroyer, and I watch the little group on her quarterdeck until the refrain has ended and the figures have disappeared into the darkness. I hear a step behind me.

"From the Captain, sir. Will you please go down to the wardroom and drink the New Year in?"